YOU OPEN A DOOR AND IT'S A STARRY NIGHT

other books by the author

POETRY
Dawn Visions
Burnt Heart/Ode to the War Dead
This Body of Black Light Gone Through the Diamond
The Desert is the Only Way Out
The Chronicles of Akhira
The Ramadan Sonnets
The Blind Beekeeper
Mars & Beyond
Laughing Buddha Weeping Sufi
Salt Prayers
Ramadan Sonnets (The Ecstatic Exchange revised edition)
Psalms for the Brokenhearted
I Imagine a Lion
Coattails of the Saint
Abdallah Jones and the Disappearing-Dust Caper
Love is a Letter Burning in a High Wind
The Flame of Transformation Turns to Light
Underwater Galaxies
The Music Space
Cooked Oranges
Through Rose Colored Glasses
Like When You Wave at a Train and the Train Hoots Back at You
In the Realm of Neither
The Fire Eater's Lunchbreak
Millennial Prognostications
You Open a Door and it's a Starry Night

THEATER/ THE FLOATING LOTUS MAGIC OPERA COMPANY
The Walls Are Running Blood
Bliss Apocalypse

PROSE
Zen Rock Gardening
The Little Book of Zen
Zen Wisdom

YOU OPEN A DOOR
AND IT'S A STARRY NIGHT

POEMS

OCTOBER 29, 1997 - MAY 23, 1998

DANIEL ABDAL-HAYY MOORE

The Ecstatic Exchange
2009
Philadelphia

You Open a Door and it's a Starry Night
Copyright © 2009 Daniel Abdal-Hayy Moore
All rights reserved.
Printed in the United States of America

For quotes any longer than those for critical articles and reviews, contact:
The Ecstatic Exchange,
6470 Morris Park Road, Philadelphia, PA 19151-2403
email: abdalhayy@danielmoorepoetry.com

First Edition
ISBN: 978-0-578-01004-5 (paper)
Published by *The Ecstatic Exchange*,
6470 Morris Park Road, Philadelphia, PA 19151-2403

Also available from *The Ecstatic Exchange:*
Knocking from Inside, poems by Tiel Aisha Ansari

Cover collage by the author
Back cover photograph by Peter Sanders

DEDICATION

To
Shaykh ibn al-Habib
(and the continuation of the Habibiyya)
Shaykh Bawa Muhaiyuddeen,
all shuyukh of instruction and ma'arifa
and
Baji Tayyaba Khanum
of the unsounded depths

✣

*The earth is not bereft
of Light*

CONTENTS

The Great Escape   11
My Hard Head   13
Not Enough   15
Monologue   18
Words   22
A Fable   25
Ulele Ulele   27
Who Taught Who What   29
Quicksilver   31
The Old Teacher   32
The Green Man   35
Trade Off   38
Glimpses   41
Love's Icy Glow   42
If I Told You   45
Cabin   48
The Ridiculous   50
Take Down the Universe   52
The Poem   55
There's a Rose in This World   58
Homage to the Discoverers   60
Old Man of the Sea   63
Ovidian Beasts   65
Turquoise   70
Shaving Lesson   72
To a Titanic Passenger Who Decided
    to Go Down with the Ship   74
Train Scene   78

Tiny Man   82
Stone Crackjaw   84
The Sexual Lives of Moths   86
Paradoxes   88
Hit   90
Address   91
He Waved Goodbye   92
Surrounded by Incomprehension   94
On the Thin Magisterial Borderline   96
Blue Darkness   98
Signs of the End   100
Small Bits of Advice   102
Simple Questions   104
Down a Long Shadowed Alleyway   106
Fairy Tale   108
The Spark   110
Horse   112
Past Midnight   115
Soap the Button   117
From the Peak   119
We Blink   121
The Djinn in the Box   123
Dictation   125
One Day   127
The Truth is Revealed   129
In-Breath Out-Breath   131
The Tower in the Lake   133
Home For the Owl   135
Games   136
Driving in Silence   137
Checklist   139

The Face of God Direct   142
Novel   145
Teachers and the Teaching   148
Looking for Signs   152
Perpetual Motion   154
Down into the Pool   157
Rachel, Magdalene, Celeste and Brooker   159
Figures of Speech   161
The Feeling of Welcome   163
Fortune Cookie   165
In These Bodies   167
In a Poem   172
Death Curves Inward   174
Flower Show   176
Five Minutes to Live   180
Quail in the Grass   182
Red   184
How to Extend the Poem from the Body   187
After a Dream   189
Archipelagos   191
You Open a Door and it's a Starry Night   194
Small Parable   197
To Proclaim His News   198
Of My Mother, 92, with Alzheimers   200
Mockingbird Outside My Window   206
Jerusalem   208
Recording Angels   211
Due Proportion   213
Traces   215
Behemoth in the Mouth   217
Leaves   219

Gravity 220
On Tour 222
The Poet's Vision 224
How it Comes 225
How the Universe Works 228
Remember Your Origin and Goal 230
Why I Want Li-Young Lee to Send Me the Poem
    He Read to Me Over the Telephone 232
Lunar Day 234
All My Life 235
Ocean Poetry 237
Conscious Thought Processes 240
Love's Not Meant to be Easy 242
A Poetics 244
Roses of Time 246
Sheep of the Night 248

So you want to go away from me? Well, it's a decision as good as any other. But where do you mean to go? Where is this away-from-me? On the moon? It is not even there, and anyway you will never get so far. And so why then all this? Wouldn't you rather sit down in the corner and be quiet. Wouldn't that, for instance, be better? There in the corner, warm and dark? You aren't listening? Groping for the door. Yes, but where is there a door? So far as I recall there is none in this room. Who at that time, when this place here was being built, thought of such world-shaking plans as yours are? Well, nothing is lost, such an idea does not get lost, we shall discuss it at the round table, and may the laughter be your reward.

— Franz Kafka (*The Fourth Notebook*)

THE GREAT ESCAPE

He sits without arms and legs
on an iceberg in the middle of the night.

His heart gives off an incandescent glow.

One star in particular seems to stand
directly above him.

His memories swirl.

Out of the night a door opens.
There's yellow light in a rectangle around it.

Legs come for him.
He stands on them and walks.

Arms surround him and become
attached. His face is revealed.

He walks through the door to where
his memories become thin as thread
and his eyesight acute.

He can make out
the opposite shore.

His heart becomes clear.

A pine tree grows from its shoot

where he sat.

He's no longer here.

10/29

MY HARD HEAD

A shrill bell is heard
but it's a door slamming.

The sound of a pin dropping,
but it's two trains crashing.

The sound of a full choir singing its heart out,
but it's thirty braying asses on hills of
olive trees in Sardinia.

The sound of burning
but it's my heart longing to enter
dimensions where
things are revealed in their
purest essences, where

the long shadows of intangibility are
no longer cast across everything, or rather

the true light of reality shines from its
source onto everything that
moves or is quiet, everything that's
thought or movement in the heart,

and the open, singing sound of
everything is heard loud and
clear, instead of the sound of

constant hammering and the driving of

nail into cement wall,

and it's my head, O Lord,
it's my hard head,

hammer, nail *and* wall!

10/30

NOT ENOUGH

There's always this nagging feeling
   that being mortal isn't enough.
Going up the icy mountain inside through years of
   daily life isn't enough.
Getting worn out with cares and worries
   watching your children grow up and
      run out into traffic
         isn't enough.

Letting go and holding on, letting all those
love letters go like flocks of wild
   doves over ruined rooftops
      isn't enough.
Sailing across the sky in hope and desire
or falling out of the sky with anguish finally getting the
   better of you
      isn't enough.

Watching some die and some get born
   isn't enough.
Looking out across the great gray bay waters
as one season comes right after another year after year
isn't enough.

Flaming poles rise up from zebra plains,
clouds of fire float among glass houses,
memories flit through like ghosts
   wearing ski masks,

cold nights in which devotion is a blue flame
   that warms an entire city,
orange mist that swims across black sky,
echoes of the names of the great who have
   emptied themselves of their
      precious jewels and died, leaving
         their shines behind,

the black horse of beauty, the white horse of
   death,

my wife of warmth who cools my erupting rages,
the length of a life unreeling its coil
   moment by moment, dropping us
  further and further

     down an abyss or raising us
higher and higher into an actual starry firmament,

imagery as clever as a newspaper, as
   colorful as Tibetan tankas
      flickering behind butter lamps,

all the avenues and byways we
   go up in search of the
lost blind bird of our eager spiritual youth
or the chattering wind-up toy that first showed us
   delight in the world –

but the world keeps showing us old horror films
where it stars as the old toothless hag or the

    mad scientist with solid white hair, we're
not meant to depend on it too heavily or
find it too terribly attractive –

it isn't enough, none of it is enough,
our aches and pains aren't enough, our
    great good natures aren't
      enough, unless we

tip the golden chalice into our lips, unless we
actually ride the white horse of
  death, unless we
    walk through the
shattering glass houses of memory or eat the
fire of our lives backwards that we
ignited forwards, unless we
open our burning eyes like
crystals in skies of bright blue
velvet in truly
  innocent atmospheres,

it isn't enough.

It isn't enough to just sit in a room
burning with heart's desire.

It isn't enough.

                            11/4

MONOLOGUE

1

A cheap suit, a ringing
 pain in my teeth, a
book whose pages keep bursting into flame
    whenever I try to read them – *this is
the life, and I
wouldn't trade it for anything!*

I leave the door open
and everyone walks out!

I slide into a store to buy a new blue handkerchief
and stagger out with this
mahogany bedroom set and a
    black eye!

The fact that the saxophone player was
    way off key shouldn't have
been a problem to anyone but me –
    it was *my* song!

The fact that the forest was closing in and
no one saw it coming
shouldn't have been a big surprise,
    we all get a little
greedy, then a little paranoid, then
a little itchy and anxious to leave. And
why don't we? The

land's for sale, and your
in-laws never paid off the
mortgages on the feather boa factory or the
   glass cage on the hill.

*And just now when the demand for feather boas
   is so high!*

I feel like a freight train's
crushing me. The one with all my
photo albums in big wooden boxes. And
homeless people sleeping in the corridors.
Clickety-clack, clickety-clack!

Just waiting for that call,

   that rendezvous with a
burning love that will
   boil my pocket change.

Why else make footsteps?
Why else cast a shadow?

Don't yell out now, the
newest members of the
human paradigm are sleeping!

Meow if you
can read this!

I'm off the deep end

next to a pissing horse.
But did you
notice the wing-spread on him?

Say hello to my ma
if she comes back around.

Say hello to your Aunt Fanny.

2

OK. Everything I've just said
is only half the story.
One half of the other half
is like a subway station in the
   dead of winter, with
everyone waiting to go home.

The other half is gold steps disappearing into
   the Empyrean. There are
little herds of deer there, and a
   high-pitched ringing sound.

But I go from being well fed to
wrenched with hunger.

You can't say everything twice
quite the same way! *You can't even
   say it once!*

Look, the guy with the green hair
    says the end is near.
We all get a little crazy when he
    talks that way.

One kiss in the shadow of the roller coaster
and I'm out of here.
I think we're taking this
way too seriously. And at the
same time
not seriously enough!

Say your prayers, Maggie.
Fish are beginning to fly!
Holy Mackerel are
   coming back as
      black roses!

If you say you saw me
make sure you say there
   was no one there.

Here's my card: *The Ace of Spades.*

The wind keeps
blowing my face off!

If you say you saw me
say nothing.
The sky will reply.

11/8

WORDS

"It's a rotten shame," said the strangler
   as he watched the last
      bubbles ascend.

"We're all doomed," said the balloonist
   as the hissing sound grew louder.

"We've arrived, I think," thought the subaqueous
    geologist, fathoms deep, at the
central rift.

"One more bend!" shouted the jockey, and
Butterfly McQueen's black ears silkily
     twitched.

"One thousand, two thousand," thought the
    chemist, as the
  gold liquid rose in the glass.

"A billion of us more than we should be,"
mused the geneticist ironically to her
    assistant.

"I'm letting myself down slowly," mouthed
   the mountaineer descending Everest to
himself, blue lips quivering icily.

*"Homespun is nice, but dynamite is
   quicker,"* said the

blond sociopath to his black boyfriend.

"We've all got as long as it
takes to sip water," said the twinkly-eyed
    guru to his disciples, laughing.

"I think all my time has passed," thought
the dying soldier in the trench, tears
    dropping on his rifle butt.

"The doors are closed, but the walls are opening,"
    said the enigmatic soothsayer to the
small Lithuanian crowd gathered in his room.

"Blue bells are blooming, but I won't be there,"
said my mother as she lay down the
    receiver, distracted.

"Seven thousand strangers, and I
never knew any of them," said the
aging photographer pouring through his archive.

"I've sung this song to no one in
    particular," said the old partially
paralyzed poet strumming his electric lyre.

"Even birds express their gratitude,"
    said the pre-Socratic prophet to the
townspeople leaning forward to hear him.

"If we could say goodbye to

everyone with perfect equanimity, it'd be
   a perfect world for sure," said the blind
philosopher, sagging, his
   words resounding and then
     resounding again around the
      turquoise tiled dome
   of the empty chamber.

"Shhhhhh, it'll all be over soon," said the
criminal to the sobbing executioner, who
   suddenly felt compassion as he
     swung his axe on high. It
caught a flash from the sun and its light
extended through time to the present moment.

*"I've just arrived, but I've got to
go,"* said the oblivious Homo sapiens
   barely used to his
     earthly shadow.

"The earth fits into my breast pocket," said the
   mystic, his spirit expanding to
     engulf every galaxy.

"You smell like chrysanthemums," said the
   doctor to the patient
suddenly returning from a three month coma.

"I saw God naked in the inner garden," said
the patient to the doctor leaning over him,
   dying of cancer, smiling.

A FABLE

He picked up his pen and
   threw it in the river.
It whistled as it flew.
It didn't whistle Dixie.
It whistled a tune of its
   own making
which he couldn't hear.
It was out of earshot.
It flew over the
   river and cast a
snaky shadow.
He had flung it far from him.

Why write anymore?
Birds were too busy
   singing to listen.
The air was thick with
   birdsong.
People were far too
   busy to bother.
The traffic of busy people was
often unbearable.

Eternity came in tickable chunks
and its seductive breezes
   did lick his face now and
     then, but in
impatience he flung his pen into the
   river.

The rustling waters covered it over.
Their little rushing strands wove over and
   under.
They carried it along in its liquid basket.
It almost sang a nursing song, a
   mother's melody as it
swept the pen along.

It swept down the river.
A poor boy sat by the river
   brokenhearted over
something or other.

He thought it was
   one thing, but it was
probably another.
Suddenly he saw the
   pen float by.
It gleamed like a small trout.
He leaned into the river and
fished it out. It
   shone in the sunlight.

He pulled out a piece of crumpled
   paper he had
and began to write.

His words made song like the
   birdsong around him.
He wrote all night.

11/15

ULELE ULELE

1

A heaven of houses, each
  mounted on a wheel.
They roll down a hill
  and out across an icy sky.

Out of each window
  a singer leans and sings.
Hundreds of singers in
  three-part harmony.

One's named Gladys. One is
Melody. One is James of the Clear Eye.

One has a noble red beard like a
waterfall. His name is Lank.
He harmed no one
and saw that the doors were secure.
His mother leans out a distant
  window but her voice is
soft and well-woven into the harmony.

The song unrolls like a long
  satin ribbon.
Shadows of migrating birds and
butterflies flutter across it.

It flaps in the windless air.

2

"Ulele ulele," they sing, oblivious to the wheeling falcons.
"We are earnest in what we do," they say to themselves
underneath their breath. Song
    covers it. It is their
      flesh. Without song
their bones would walk off.

Only a very bright light would remain.

Hardy and savage, they strike up
   again in a higher register.
"Ulele ulele," happily
as small boats filled with
   fluffy children cross a still
     lake in bright sunlight.
Their faces are clean and bright. They
look up and wave, and the singers
   sing suddenly louder, directing their
     voices to them rather than
to just anywhere in a wide compass, hoping
      angels will hear.

"Ulele ulele," the song goes
   out across the lake
making the children clap their hands
   with glee.

"Ulele ulele."

11/17

WHO TAUGHT WHO WHAT

The eagle taught the rabbit
  how to keep out of sight.

The bear taught the trout
  how to slip away.

The elephant taught its mahout
  how to scrub its back.

The dwarf taught the growing boy
  how to look tall.

The window taught the wall
  how to be more transparent.

The floor taught the roof
  how to be more down to earth.

The water taught the wine
  how to be always clear-headed.

The wine taught the water
  how to throw off all restraints.

The earth taught the blind man
  how to see with his feet.

The wind taught the toupee
  how to be more truthful.

The rainbow taught our hearts
   how to expect more of the unseen.

The bridge taught the river
   how to overcome obstacles.

The mule taught the townspeople
   how to put up with its braying.

The lovers taught each other
   how to accept each other's faults.

Darkness taught daylight
   how to wait until it's time.

The body taught the soul
   not to rely on it forever.

                                                   11/20

QUICKSILVER

The windows fill with an odd light for
   this time of day, a green
     light like a
shaft from Paradise comes into the
   field of vision like a
     herd of young gazelle bounding across
        savannas in Africa

then leap up and blend into
the blue and are gone.

Quicksilver fills the window like a sky that is
so saturated with light everything that
flies in it disappears in it.

Our hearts are drawn into the
golden element as well as the
   fiery element, but

hold firm to words which, when
put together, construct a bridge

over the abyss.

                                            11/22

THE OLD TEACHER

The old teacher looked at us with
   great sad eyes.
He had something of the look of an old
   cypress tree about him. You'd
swear there were squirrels
leaping in his hair.

His hands lay on shards of earth,
platters of continents, bits of land mass
with cobras and exotic orchids. Arctic
   banks shining ice blue in
     the surrounding waters.

Shadows thicker than the skulkings of war,
deeper than the thoughts of lone voyagers on the
   high seas after months away from
     shore.

Mouth open, but no words coming out,
instead, pictures, animated, pictographs,
   illuminated, icons with Gothic
     light all around them,
and he sighed.

He was the one who taught us life and death,
life in death and death in life.

At his chin was the origin of the Nile,
at his throat, Victoria Falls.

Birds with wide black wingspread flew across the
   opening.

His clear blue eyes, silver-blue, didn't blink.
Looking into his fathomless pupils, we saw
  migrations as far back as the
    Neolithic, across
natural bridges, bringing their
  weapons and canoes.

He had no books. When he
turned his hands palms down
  night fell.
When he opened his palms
light spread. And the lines of his hands
were vocables, syllables, stops and formations
from every possible sound made
into comprehensible speech.

But he remained silent.
He didn't need to speak. His
  face spoke for him.

And we took into our hearts what we
took, and like nutrients in food,
assimilated it and made it
  our own.

Breathed more easily knowing he'd
  been there before us, was
    bathed in the presence of

a Compassionate God. And

now gazed at us with
perfect equanimity.

Gazed at us like
someone we'd never see.

11/23

THE GREEN MAN

"If you're waiting for lightning to
    strike you, kid," he said, shifting his
tobacco wad to the other cheek,

"or a great voice to address you special
    from a dry riverbed, or
an animal, your cat maybe, or a large
    wingéd thing, to suddenly get a
human face and look you straight in the
eye and say something in human speech,

well, *forget it!*" He slid down from the
fence, or was it that he had just
materialized from the green hillside?

Now all the details are blurred.

"The universe isn't gonna contract to the
    size of a crystal ball you can
shake and it'll give you neat answers,

you're not gonna open a book and it'll
just start reading itself to you with a
voice, say, of Orson Welles, deep and
    stentorian, making
authoritative glances at you from the
    typeface,

you may meet a perfect person who's

walked out of the eternal fabric and
no distinction remains where they
begin and end and the whole
divine efflorescence begins and ends,

but generally," and with this he
   cocked his one good eye,
"*generally*, you're gonna havta
measure out your patience to run alongside
time itself, each drip of rainwater from the
drain around your brain will be

the great clock's tick, you're gonna havta
push the rock of your heart up the big hill all by yourself
and each day count as a hundred for

deep satisfaction, find out yourself a
good way to do dishes and wash
clothes and get along with gravity, the way things
always fall to the floor, or
crash together at the
  last minute, with
    you inside, like a
mortality sandwich!

Nah, you can't beat yourself up over this
day after day, pockets worn
  out from thrusting your bunched
fists in 'em.

Fresh air does wonders.

Brisk exercise. Keep your
heart awake with remembrance. Never let the
Name of Truth leave your tongue
   alone. Then you'll
never be alone."

He loped off. Without a
   backwards wink,

not even with his
one good eye,

not even with his bad.

                                        11/24

TRADE OFF

His senses closed down one by one and
   little by little, so that
when he began to see a little less well,
     had to squint to see distant
        street signs,

a new blond creature rose up from a distant wild savanna,
licked off its afterbirth, stretched its
face happily in the morning sun.

When ringing started in his right ear
a long-haired giraffe-like creature across the earth
     stood wobbly up,
  tried to keep its balance, its
great soft black-eyelashed eyes
       focused on its feet.

When he couldn't wiggle his arthritic fingers without a
   sharp pain flashing along his
     arm to the elbow
a lovely jellyfish, neon pink,
floated up to a moonlit surface from a
   murky depth in a distant sea and
spread out the incandescent membranes of its
   body, undulating
      ribbony tentacles across dark waters.

So that as he diminished, nerve by
tingling nerve, sight by growing

blindness, acute
hearing by a muffling loud blanket of deafness,
some totally new being somewhere,
    unique among the planets, rose
up like a bubbling thought through
      amorphousness to
        silhouette clarity, stretched its

living heartbeats in space as his
own heartbeats grew dim.

When something slipped his mind
a distant piano started playing
    enchanted music.

When he said something foolish he'd have
never said before
a fanning of bright yellow moth wings took
   place in a dark part of a forest
      somewhere, delighting a mud-splattered
        child of three.

As his life became overcast by his
    gradual failings, his
shutting down extension by sensual
    extension into the world,
withdrawing into the leafier landscapes of
his innermost self, shadow nooks with
    pools, water dripping from a
great black height onto a surface clear as
        blue velvet,

his heart, invisible even to the most
powerful electron microscope,

opened like a seismic rift in the most ancient ocean floor

and all his inner senses came alive as if played by
   xylophone fingertips with
      glass-clear resonance,

and he entered a darkness blindingly intense,

and a silence that dropped into
mute harmonies so deep

no natural canyon could contain them.

11/25

GLIMPSES

Confronted with insurmountable problems,
he turned into a butterfly.

Firing his rounds one after another at the
police, he thought of his mother.

The black cat was so comfortable on the
rug, her face sank down into it
and disappeared.

Filling the grocery bag to the top with
groceries, the clerk said, *"Blue antelopes
fresh from Brazil."*

Happy at last, in a two piece suit and a
gallery full of his paintings, he
died of a heart attack.

Thoroughly involved in how the race was
going, she didn't notice she was
pulling the one hair of the bald man in front of her.

Lost in thought, imagining his glory,
the chemist was oblivious to the
spark jumping to the floor.

LOVE'S ICY GLOW

Love's all I've got,
   roof over my head,
ground underfoot,
space of light we'll all be lowered in,
sharp glass corners of the universe
shaken by lightning flashes of love.

Outside red and blue planets
  held in elliptical orbits by
love's forces, spun on
    dizzying axes by
love's motions, whirled in love's
     atmospheres. It

drips through atoms of matter
like water through coffee grounds,
   making the
     perfect blend.
We sip with heads tilted back, eyes
    flights of white geese,
hearts like thunder.

Love calls to a soldier about to
   step on a mine.
He's saved intact.
Trembles in gratitude
three days, no eating or sleeping,
  wove tight in love's web.
Love blows another into a million

pieces, releasing his
      soul in a fusillade of
fireworks, each
spinning fragment an ecstatic universe blown into
      space, his happy
spirit singing new songs enough to make
snow lift from the ground and
return intact to its source, each
      perfect flake
   falling back into the fiery eye of love
stretched out above the night.

Love broaches no argument.

Sizzles on a platter and draws
blood with each breath.

Watches as stampeding wildebeests
pour like water across a plain,
     hooves making one
   single roar as of
one hoof booming through the earth.

Love waits till the patient is totally hopeless,
appears at bedside with disguise removed,
   naked as ice, gazing right in his
eyes to make
obvious what was only an inkling before,
one or two keys on the keyboard
now become the entire plenitude of sound held down
with both hands and loud pedal

    echoing to heaven.
Love's the noose and the horseman and
round clouds across China.
It's the gourmet's laughing ground,
ultimate taste sensation that makes
    everyone glad.

It's thrown in the air like handfuls of confetti,
each piece the space into which it was
    thrown, space within space,
each glimpse of
sky through these eyes the entire sky these
    eyes find visible,

until love's pure stillness soothes our
frantic angles into one
slim repose under aurora borealis
light curtains shivering endlessly

in love's icy glow.

                                                11/29

IF I TOLD YOU

If I told you God was a black beetle
   looking down at us from a glassy horizon,
or a white shirt freshly pressed, left nonchalantly
   on the back of our chair,

if I said God was a volcanic rush in a column
   of incandescence, bright orange,
giant vertical blast of light from one spot
   in the middle of the earth,

if I said God sat in a billion veils on a
   chair that melts and unmelts each second,
or the fuel of lightning and breath sufficient for
   tiny gnats as well as fat potentates,

if I said God was a brown-skinned woman sitting
   alone in a narrow chamber,
or a speaking rod someplace in the desert, flung
   on the ground amidst miles of sand,

if I said God rose up from the bottom of the sea, waves
   recoiling from the girth of His shoulders,
a stone slowly rolling from the top of a mountain,
   mossless, noiseless, toward the village below,

the air turned black in the middle of day,

the power of catastrophe where everyone's killed,

a lacy blue wildflower on a cliff on Mt. Everest,

a green smoke emitted from a cave in Cathay,

if I told you God was a human-faced beast
    roaming invisibly from city to city

then would you believe, would the
hairs on your neck bristle, your
throat go dry, your heart thump
    audibly?

Ah, drunken friends, that would be too easy!
God's none of these:
a blast of goodness, a

    thunderous voice,
an inner impression of monumentality,
a vague sensation, an inkling of grandeur,
    a benevolent despot who
    distributes fate like
marked playing cards or ominous dominos
        clacking.

After miles of words trying to define God,
the best we can do is just keep silent.

Stand still in a doorway, stay
calm in a lightning flash.

Lie on our beds and listen to a clock tick.

Sit and face miles and miles of blank wall.

Drink cold water direct from a spring.

But that's still not it!

12/3

CABIN

I wake up with this image of a little
   wooden cabin in my head,
shack on a hillside, woods,
    a little lopsided structure
      with black window,
but maybe it's from hearing the defense
lawyers for the Unibomber are having his cabin
transported from its woods to the courtroom
to show he's a lunatic
  (though killing people through letter bombs
      might be the real tipoff),

"Ladies and gentlemen of the court, how do you
think it would be to live in this
tiny room day after day, the sun beating
  down, the rain beating
    down, racoons all
around, eating out of cans?"

Or perhaps I'm just thinking of archetype
   shelters of woodsy liberation,
cabin in the sky, cabin of my
   heart on a hill among free-flying
      birds.
Maybe it wasn't a cabin at all, but a
   box kite cutting loose from its
string and shuddering away.

Where will my heart hide from

this world's sinister blows
    without that

roof over my head?

                                                        12/4

THE RIDICULOUS

I climb out of my tossed bed of ridiculousness,
put on my ridiculous rhododendron shirt,
slip on my ridiculous blue shoes.
Geese are flying with little ridiculous hats.
Light from another room
   spills at a ridiculous angle onto
     my dark Zebra floor.
Vistas out my ridiculous window
go way beyond being simply ridiculous:
the bread man with a long French loaf on his handlebars,
Siamese policemen with white gloves directing traffic,
fish so far down in the depths of the ocean they
have to have little Dr. Seuss headlamps
   sprouting from their noses.

Of course, Lord, maybe it's just me.
Maybe everyone else walks around
   the epitome of sobriety,
the ridiculous smile on my face simply part of a
   Mr. Potato head ensemble.

OK. If I wander off the main road
I enter ridiculous territory, that I know,
but certainly it's not usual for pairs of
   Pekinese dogs to say
"good morning" in perfect synchronized English,
or bagels to start wearing their
   holes on the outside.

I don't even know what that means!

*Stop the avalanche of minor circus performances,
I came here for the main event!*

An Italian submarine emerging
with crew safely inside eating
   mayonnaise sandwiches!

The Apocalyptic eclipse!

Survivors all wearing
real smiles of gratitude!

My own,
burned indelibly into my face!

12/11

TAKE DOWN THE UNIVERSE

Take down the universe bit by bit,
dismantle its brute manifestos,
  cancel the President's breakfast in the
Van Buren Room, on the Roosevelt table, by the
  Zachary Taylor fireplace,
demote the ambitious CEO pinstripe by pinstripe,
  unthreading his intricate
    signature on checks and contracts with a
similar but reverse flourish,

call in all Greek fishing boats, with or
  without catch, the handsome young
oarsmen dreaming of buxom taverna
  waitresses in scoop-neck blouses, whistling,

call back all executive orders: *Buy! Sell!*
  Liquidate! Kill! And
erase that rat-like look of satisfaction in the
eyes of the slavish underlings who would
love to carry them out,

return all glasses, broken or unbroken, to
  The Management, lipstick or not
    on their rims, drinks finished or
      unfinished,

let all fruits and vegetables picked for
  world consumption
    return to their stems,

    tree boughs, stalks, branches,
  twinkling again in the respectable
      rawness of real sunlight,

return all zoo animals to their natural habitats,
lemurs, wild-eyed, amazed and
    a little disoriented to be
      back home instead of in
concrete cages with one ramp and a
      single-nailed tree bough,

let the high and outrageously higher notes
return to their sopranos, their mezzo sopranos, their
    coloraturas with their grueling
      study and practice since childhood,

return each painstaking note to its
  silent source under the larynx's unknown
      grottos and reservoirs,

return the diamonds, zirconium and
  all dubious emeralds in reality true
      gems back to their
earthy beds, cool to the cheek of them,
covered over again by the sediment of time,

whirl all planetary motions back and
   back into the oblong serene, the
     octagonal octave of undressed
joy before the unstopping gaze of firstness,
everything fresh, new, before stretching, before

first heartbeat-ticks,

it's over, it's time to just stand still, let all
worlds slam back into their generating
  chests, heartbone
    serenade, voice dumb,
mind vacant as the North Pole,
just the tiny sound of the scrunch of
     clean snow underfoot, the

darkness blowing back onto our faces like the
winds of discovery when the great
explorers rounded bends and saw
   Victoria Falls for the
first time, the Pacific Ocean, the
  first teenage kiss on a
   back porch late
    September, brisk
  in the chill air of oncoming winter,

let the whole thing fall back into itself, fold
up into its carrying case across
  illimitable stretches of space, let

Johnny the young artilleryman carry it, carefully,
between land mines, let it
down slowly, let it very

slowly and carefully down.

THE POEM

I would write poems that withstand an
   infinity of readings, deep and
multi-layered with multiple meanings, transparencies
floating across transparencies as
   simple as a sunny day, that as you

go down them little mossy trap doors fall open, rivers
fan out into chasms of energy and tremendous
hydraulic power, legends present themselves in
   silken costumes that
flutter away with their legends inside them,

and as you go down a natural corridor, maybe even one you
feel you've been down before,

suddenly huge new vistas rear up like those
early giant paintings of the far West with
   golden light pouring down
faces of equally golden cliffs,

waterfall roar throbbing its bass notes
momentous to our ears.

Great oceanic waves of light should wash over its lines
from time to time, transforming readers into doves,
   resistance into houses filled with revelers,
hatred into fires burning peacefully at the
      outskirts of town.

God would look in at one of the windows at least
once, and be recognized. A white
horse might step out of a wall and stand
with its flanks twitching excitedly in a
half-darkened room.

The poem might be a comfortable
   gallery overlooking a canyon
where intoxicating drinks like rainbows
    are served from conch-shell trays,

or at the far edge of an
inhospitable desert where new
   visions of the universe and our
      reasons for being in it
stretch across the sky in
   panoramas of raw magnificence.

Also ticking like a trusted clock by your side.
Purring like a 1940's automobile, with
   roomy trunk space and
     hard rubber running boards.

The readers transformed into doves might
fly into nearby branches and coo,
or they might land on gravestones and
bring a certain poignancy to death,

a strange light
shining in their eyes,

a strong pink dawn
pushing down a very black sky.

                                                    12/16

THERE'S A ROSE IN THIS WORLD

There's a rose in this world
   I won't call it a name
they seek to find it
   it eludes their sight

At the edge of things
   is a furtive light
to help in their search
   it will do them no good

This flower not a flower
   blooms unseen in a space
we breathe its domain
   we wear its face

It walks in blue wind
   it speaks with leaves
its eyes are intense
   with desire for our lives

This rose seeks us
   but doesn't leave its root
the air transmits
   its aroma to us

Being careful and true
   is part of its allure
wild cries in the night
   are part of its purity

How can we see it
   through its medium we gaze
at itself revolving
   slowly in our sight

It is so far off
   it couldn't be nearer
hear its thump in the blood
   hear its name spoken softly

Indescribable rose
   all try to describe you
you'd not die if we didn't
   you'd not live if we did

12/18

HOMAGE TO THE DISCOVERERS

Aroo, the short man with slight limp
who discovered the lengthening and
shortening of shadows throughout the day,

Kafnaa, woman of straight black hair and
  slim pointed breasts who saw the way to add
water to sifted flour to make sun-baked bread,
and her sister Poona who
  flattened the lumps and laid them on
    smooth hot rocks just after sunrise.
Poona also seemed to understand
    the language of cats.

Horgnath, elegantly supple and lightly
  muscled, who found a way to
sit on a horse's back and soothe it into
going where he wanted, squeezing his
  thighs and making those
    clucking and clicking noises with his
tongue you hear horse-trainers use today.

Bazna Snarr, who found that by cupping her
mouth with her hands as she stood on a
  rocky outcrop her voice carried
    a little farther to Shnoog waiting on
the opposite cliff, cupping his ear the same way,
  nearly out of sight behind a
    stand of tall pines,

Tash, who made the discovery that a
   crushed bug never walks,
Tos, that water poured onto an incline will
   roll down it rather than
     stay in a puddle on its angle
(certainly the spiritual and probable
   genetic ancestor to Newton millenniums later),

Oolash, who found that by putting berries
   between two rocks and squeezing, he'd
     get juice, of course he
had to lick the rocks, receptacles discovered not
   until some time later, by

Shla, by making a depression in soft clay
with an egg, preferably a petrified egg,
then letting the clay sit in the sun until hard,
then catching the juice as
   discovered by Oolash that runs down an
incline as discovered by Tos, and
raising the clay cup of juice to
Chief Katoosh, a form of celebration

discovered by Yoloff one twilight
   evening under an
     aurora borealis sky,

ah, all these are our ancestors in discovery
the way babies discover staircases and
   hot pans, sunlight on their
     faces and

mosquito bites,

and their active shadows still fall this far
along in time –
Jaja who discovered that by
sitting on a flat piece of bark he could
　　toboggan down a hill,

Smoonash who discovered that by putting
a small block of ice (even better splattered with
fresh berry juice) on a stick,
　　he had the first popsicle,

or Laniah who saw the figures and objects
　in dreams and knew they had
　　sinister or positive import,

firstness and freshness being the
key to our own lightheartedness

while a mushroom cloud rises behind us
and technological doom gently
　　tugs at our clothes

to sit down among its discoveries

like looming
shadows on a wall.

12/19

OLD MAN OF THE SEA

Sunny lanes along the curvature of the
earth in space, window

boxes of pink-red geraniums tended by
slender girls in blue gowns, endlessly

variegated subdivisions of space by objects that
cast actual shadows, especially on

white stucco surfaces, the hot breath of
the sun itself on the bright side of this orb,

also at sea, the light, the heat, the sound of
sky and ever-changeable sea, and out of the

sea itself, Proteus, Old Man of the Sea, wrestled to
transform into rock, stag, house, harlot,

Singapore train station, gabbing
talk show host, tree, spindly tree full of stars,

wide-spreading elm against the entire heavenly
bowl, with all the starry bodies themselves outlining

their vanishing mythical characters, then finally
the old guy, laying among his blubbery

seals also sunning themselves, salt sliding
off their slick sides, he casts an

old salt eye on us, the old man, lifts his
kelp-haired head as if to indicate something out

there in the middle of nowhere, then
slyly slides out of grip back into the

sea again, another sunny
escapade, swindler, things-as-they-are,

leaving their impression
long after they're gone,

idle never, sidewinders, we are
alone. Oh God, without You

we founder, we cannot find nor
fathom who we are.

12/21

OVIDIAN BEASTS

1

If I put my hand to my face and found
a horny beak instead of a nose
with feather tufts above it, and a
    feathery brow, or if I

touched my forehead and brushed against
something that blinked and had eyelashes, the
    famous Third Eye actually dwelling there
outwardly, all-seeing, for all to see!

Or touched my lips to brush away a crumb and found
a cat's thin lips and sand-papery tongue,
round furry chin beneath, button nostrils,

went to scratch my head and felt a
coarse beast-mane long-hanging and shaggy,

or extended, Kafka-like, my leg in the
morning past my bedclothes and found a
hoof instead of a foot, cloven, already
    prancing,

or emerged from the shower with wide shoulders as of
mandrill or buffalo, hunched and powerful,

would I be any less strange, any less
odd, putting on trousers, shirt and tie to go

    out into polite society not just a

metamorphosing Ovidian beast from a much more
savage place, capable of guttural shouts and
earth-shattering growls, but also with

green eyes fixed on observatory-dome-like silver-blue
skylines in which miraculous things take place
midair, hovering, windows

transpiercing our daily social intercourse with

flying creatures of all shapes and sizes, angelic or
    djinn-like, so that if I
put hand to face and find no features, or
fantastic features no human
    possesses, I won't be
      surprised,

or at least not too surprised, we're all really
strangers here in the shadow of the Light with our
    strange ways, and go,
wings back and claws in socks, down
streets with the impassive expressions of
the vaguely satisfied,

the preoccupied and distracted expressions on our
faces of the partially fulfilled.

2

I don't look anything the way I think I look.
I think I have a bird-like countenance,
    quick and plumaged, strong
eagle eyes, noble and sleek head
    emerging from a ruff of black feathers, but
fleshier, less intense, a bit more
    normal looking than my
inner projection that gets no further than my
    own imagination. Mirrors

flash some stranger my way, whom I
    smile at as if to indicate
peaceful coexistence, but it's
really someone else, freeloader
        stringing along.

Where I imagine more
Wagnerian, the look is more
Ionesco. Rather than
gallantly heroic, more bourgeois. And
hair has a lot to do with it.

Or, taking off from certain photos of me, there are
times, with certain very short haircuts, even
    buzz cuts, where a
crazed Trotskyite terrorist look comes to
mind, or is
    in my mind at least, something
infinitely more

dangerous than the real thing, un-
   predictable, and
capable of mayhem. While in

actuality this face supposedly mine is
   more the face of someone
who walks his big dog, at night, under a
   street lamp, while in
actuality I have no dog and wouldn't be caught
dead walking it if I did. I

wonder how close other people's outer and
inner images of themselves mesh,
if Napoleon thought he looked like
   Alexander the Great, and if
Alex thought he resembled the sphinx, and
who the sphinx thought she
   resembled, lunar and
catlike on the
   open desert, extending those
paws, rain or
      shine?

My eyes hurt this
early in the morning, and my
face feels sore from merely
   existing. The one I

put forward. My best face.

Though maybe not

the real one. The real one
bursts into blue flame from time to time, roars
  like a lion with translucent
bronze cheeks and wide agate eyes
and a radiant

Blakean intensity!

                                                            12/23

TURQUOISE

for Sonia Gilbert

Inside its frame
The liquification of flame
Is frozen.
Outside its border
The liquid of order.
— *Stan Rice*

There's a certain quality to turquoise, especially
   when it's set in silver.
When I see it in a Navajo necklace or on a
    Tibetan long horn inlaid in brass
      or copper, I'm suddenly
somewhere else, at a high altitude, under an
open sky. It's as if it's been

chipped off one of the precious tiles of heaven, or a flake
   from a heavenly tablet, and if we could
just see the entire thing maybe
everything would be instantly explained. That
utter blueness! Like frozen water from a
lake in rock in a

place never humanly frequented, only
large black birds
   know of its existence, they
transport beads of its water in their
    beaks and occasionally
a bead falls to the ground and makes

turquoise!

Or giant beings pass in the sky with clouds moving
   aside to let them pass, clouds
     in their hair, puffy
clouds clinging to their bodies, these
corporeal beings from incorporeal dimensions,

and in the friction of their existence against the
dimension we normally exist in, sparks fly off
and become turquoise!

Hot ruby red that cools

as it falls to the ground
to make magic mirrors blue.

Blue with an air of silver in it.

Blue as if a
clear blue eye were looking through it from its
other side

directly at us!

12/24

SHAVING LESSON

I taught my son how to shave with a Bic razor
  tonight. He's twenty.
The fact that he's a full-grown child confronting
     the world for the first time
gets lost on me sometimes,
since he's so much more ready to enter the
21st Century that I am in most ways, able to
do all those famously difficult technical things
people over fifty in 1997 find so impossible,
but when it came to shaving with foam and a
non-electric razor, he was flummoxed.

So we stood in the bathroom, me bearded for
thirty straight years, only shave
clear cheek-patches and under
    chin to beard line, keeping my
moustache trimmed close and beard edges
tidy, so I

couldn't do a full demonstration, but he
wetted his face, squirted a round gob of
    too-blue gel on his
right finger and worked it into a
slimy white lather on cheeks up to his
sideburns and down to his chin. He had
two free-sample razors still in their cellophane bag,
took one out and started scraping after I
talked him through and demonstrated the downstroke.

Off came swipes of white cream with a
   few *ouched* hairs in them, *"It
pulled!"* he said. He was so
     tenuous, tentative, holding the
razor way
        up on the shank. Then I discovered these
free samples were for
heavy beards, and he's only got
wispy blond cherubic hairs, real live
    peach fuzz, so I went and
got one of my regular Bics and it worked fine.
He only got one nick. Slight. A

boy's wound. The tiny red blood
spot on his cheek from the

major war he'd won, he a

real young man facing the
mirror of his unreal reflection

standing up to it, razor in hand,
scraping off real hairs, to

face the world, with a

razor-sharp blade.

                                          12/24

TO A TITANIC PASSENGER WHO DECIDED TO GO DOWN WITH THE SHIP

Waiting for the water to drown you
   must've been the hard part, though
things moved pretty fast near the
    end, giving you little
time to make your open-hearted speech or say your
deepest inner goodbyes again, bracing yourself for the
deeps.

All the commotion. Assessing the situation.
Black sky. Black water. Cold. The air on the
deck alone only about 23 degrees or less,
except for the heat of intense excitement, everything
   so utterly genteel for the most part.
After a certain point though, after that
dawning on you of what you must do, if you
   in fact did let it dawn on you so
     clearly, maybe you
   didn't, maybe you
kept it always in the background, your
death by drowning, but if you
didn't, then after the
point of agreeing to forgo all hope of survival,
   all hope of escape or rescue, which

must have been a horrible but perhaps
    gradual realization, this
ship bigger than a tall building, longer than
   four city blocks, steam roaring, flares

flashing, men shouting, women and children
crying, pumps churning to no
    avail, the cold night, the
cold water impassively
waiting for you, when just a few moments ago, it
    seems, still vivid in your
        memory, the great

ship hurrying through a flat sea, elegant drawing
   rooms and corridors hushed, cozy,
the wonderful beveled and etched
    windows looking
out at the still night, the long polished
staircases, people in their
evening dress passing (I've put myself in the

upper class compartments, the lower class ones
     too awful to contemplate),
all that completely collapsed with the
   ripping roar of iron machinery now, the
great funnels toppling, the bow
    tipping down even more
acutely,

the stern rising evermore vertically into the sky,
your decision not even exactly final, but rather the
whole situation taken into account, the
inevitability of whatever comes,
a supernal light even coming, a real
salvation, not of this world, this
   world going down, hitting the

water, all its fine drawing rooms and bone china,
down, down, while something else
comes for you, from the same
substance as your original decision to do
   nothing to save yourself, from that

very moment now a bigger moment of real
protection, a music grander than the
tinny string sound still coming out of the
six men standing on the tilting deck and
playing, the

music of the night itself, loud innermost
    music of the disaster itself,
stars and iceberg and black icy water you're
sliding into now, music of the
deepmost essence itself pulling you down, chords in
harmony with deeps and heights
   simultaneously, with black

unfathomable iciness and your own death and
darkness, and the sky that opens up at the
same time, not sky actually, but
a real place apart from all this, only available
by going through all this, facing it

squarely, submitting completely, down to the smallest
hair fiber, down to your very atoms, your
    eyes filling with darkness,
your ears with that huge symphonic sound, your
    body freezing on contact and

being pulled down. The

mercy hitting you. The unbelievably

clear mercy of God hitting you.

Your release.

12/28

TRAIN SCENE

1

On this train car going from Trenton to New York
there are two wiry black guys whose
    voices rise above everyone else's from
        time to time, one wears a
red stocking cap and has a beard,

one very svelte woman dressed in black who was
in the bathroom when I entered the car –
she passed by me and reminded me of a
    now deceased asthmatic named Maryam
        I knew in San Antonio and later in Spain
who hoarded library books which she
constructed like walls around her in her
        room –

one big wrestler-looking dude with a stripe of
beard from underlip to chin, I first
saw him at the ticket machine in Philadelphia and
    thought *"he's only nice to his canary,"*

then across from me in the right-hand window seat
a mussy white-haired gentleman in
olive raincoat, black corduroy sweater and
    loud red scarf, professorial,
writer of history or economics textbooks, if he's a
    poet he's a formalist, no real
        innocence in his eyes,

and in the seat right in front of him, partially
    out of view, a young couple, chattery
straight-haired brunette girl, lank boy whose knees I see pressed
up against the back of the seat in
    front of him, and who
works his skinny forefinger around the
    Naugahyde seat cover as he talks –

laughter, hum of talk, a little rising
    burst from the black guys,
        distinguishable diction,
metal-creak of train wheels and
    train-car springs,
a high electric hum, heading

forward through fog and black
spindly trees, a flat white
rain-puddle heavily frequented by
seagulls standing around its edges,

a few large trucks, New Jersey
backwater scenes out the
window on my

way to New York.

2

The two black guys are actually
    astrophysicists in disguise, the one in

red stocking cap carries
    microfilm of obtuse equations proving
        the ultimate funneling of the
known and unknown universe through the
        same pinhole.
The svelte girl in black is actually a sword-swallower and
socialite from Prussia, joined a circus, defected,
and now neurotically rides the trains cross-
    country, cross-city, cross-anything.
The big wrestler-looking dude is actually a
doctor at a clinic for the poor, although he
looks mean and portly, his big hands heal
    many desperate souls of
        countless afflictions, but when he
    leaves without his white coat he looks
        just as homeless as they.
The mussy gentleman in loud red scarf
is a lyrical-spiritual poet of the highest order, who
    weeps in the depths of the night for God to
        pour radiance upon him, and who
wrote such lines as:
    "The blue window, O fill with heart's light!
    I cannot see the dawn in this broken basket!"
He stands on mountaintops above the city and
    pours his eloquence over it like
        beneficent rain.
The young couple are actually brother and
    sister, and although the boy was
        looking at a Johnny Mathis CD still
            in its wrapper, they're

dangerous killers in the mold of Bonny and Clyde,
   and their sophomoric innocence has fooled
      the entire nation from
         coast to coast.
Even I am not who I seem, I'm riding this
  train from Trenton, but actually

I'm sitting still under a silent tree at the
  edge of the Rational World
trying to attract giant
    cranes of iridescent wing who fly
back and forth in front of a
    crimson sun. It's

no wonder no one looks the same from
moment to moment.

This train's going backwards, revealing all our
innermost ways! At this rate

I'll never reach New York!

                            12/31

TINY MAN

O I'm a tiny man sitting on the
   edge of his bed on the earth at
6:30 a.m., a tiny
    gnat in the
       scheme of things,
and yet inside me is this locomotive, this
burning locomotive barreling down
   tracks billowing steam,
inside me is this boiling ocean, inside this
tiny gnat are archipelagos and wide
   Sargassos, Himalayas and
      subaqueous valleys,
clouds pass across the sky this inside is so
vast, concerts with
   grand pianos polished to
      shiny black perfection, penguins on
glaciers flapping pointy
   fins as they walk, blue
     lagoons and
dark ozones, elephantiasis and
   halitosis, Carpathian
      mountaintops and
all the Fiji Islands, I mean the

list goes on and on, and yet I
sit here on the side of my bed at 6:35 a.m.,
a tiny gnat in the scheme of things, but could
conjure up tales so dark but full of
   bright import and non-

      tragic conclusions, family
mysteries, buffooneries on the
    human condition, my eyes clicking from
side to side, Don Quixote's
    windmills turning their
        menacing arms against the
clear blue in the
ever-near Spain of my dreams,

but I sit here with notebook on knee under a
faint lamp at 6:38 a.m.,
all legs and arms and fingers on each
hand, and

inside is this locomotive, inside this

gnat-like frame is a furious black locomotive with
red face and churning wheels, silver
    smudging into rotary mist, pistons
hissing and the heavy metal couplers
    creaking, fury of forward
motion, locomotion. *Full*

steam ahead!

                                                    1/3

STONE CRACKJAW

There was this guy on Death Row, I don't
know, cop-killer, serial killer, rapist,
named Stone, Stone Crackjaw, tough,
ugly, hateful, shaped like mud, his
inner life already flames and
sharp rivers of lava,
did nothing but work out and read the papers.

Then one day he reads about this
boy who lost a kidney. He got
excited. Called his lawyer. Called the
prison doctor. Decided to
donate a kidney to save this kid's life.

Nice story. Operation successful. Now Stone's
got one kidney. It's OK, he's going to have
fried kidney anyway someday, why not
give one away!

Then he reads about this woman who needs
a lung. She's got only a few
    hours left. He's got,
who knows? Waiting for the governor,
officefuls of bureaucrats to sign papers,
then he's up in smoke anyway.
Works it out. Operation's a success. Woman
    saved. Stone's out one kidney and one lung.

He recuperates in the hospital.

Reads the paper. Bounces back in days.
Reads about this boy who needs a lobe of
liver. A nice live liver. Stone never was
much of a liver. He seems to have been more of a
dier. He gives half his liver away.
Operation successful. Later, he
gives away the other kidney. He's on
    dialysis. He's on a special diet. But he
still works out a little. Reads the
paper and waits.

Then he hears about a young doctor, someone
finding a cure for something, he's
very near victory, suddenly
struck down with a heart attack,
needs a heart quick.
Stone says, *"Take it."*

His eyes meet the surgeon's just before
anesthesia. Stone's eyes are calm. He's
looking at the world for the last time.

Gazes at his executioner.

And just past his executioner's face he sees
another. Pale. Pinkish. Bluish. With a
hint of rustling white feathers at the edges.

Seraphic.

THE SEXUAL LIVES OF MOTHS

The sexual lives of moths: what
   makes them hot? And do they get that
hot squinchy feeling we get
     when we get hot?
Various horizontal planes, plateau planes,
shale planes up steep mountain-faces,
planes at various angles, and sometimes
wild yak grazing on them. And what's a

minute to a yak? And are they
proud of their offspring?

Lilies. They blow, but do they
   know they blow?

Water lanes, curving, branching, making
wide forks as seen overhead from, say,
a helicopter or a dream. A
dream of flying coinciding with brand new
land formations. At one so

completely with the rest of creation that
our breathing out is the whole world breathing out.

And when we breathe in
inaugurations take place across the globe invisible to the
     naked eye. Inflations.

I shall not die in a standing position.

I shall not die in a sitting position.
You who barely know me, will you
    be there when I die?
One way or another? Since really

everybody is absent to our presence.
Everybody else, that is. Your

absence shall make you present,
and your presence shall
make you free.

1/5

PARADOXES

Little paradoxes, tiny little paradoxes
   arranged in a row along a
     wiry green stem attached
cunningly by its natural tendrils
   to the underside of the great palace.
Some in incongruous geometric shapes, some in
   Art Nouveau spirals, some like thick
cartoon faces being bonked by a plank,
others seductive as temptresses, almost
     ovulating with unbelievable shamelessness,
these paradoxes we live with every
moment of our existence, entangled in their
skin.

Now, they grow with the territory, the windy
territory of mortality, the very
fact of being alive and going between
   a burning house and a flooding house,
a stoic perpetrator of corporal punishment
and a Dionysian instigator of absolute license,

so that we're torn in two between
dropping our clothes in the
moonlit middle of the street embracing the
  night itself and all its charms,
or staring statuesque as if from the
    prow of a great ship entering
       foreign ports unperturbed and
         unimpressed.

I want to shout *love!* from the highest rooftops
but if I stay silent in the farthermost
    corner of the mosque
my heartbeats will sing it to the
      tune of buzzing bees and
          opening flowers.
If we drive each other mad with
indecisive encounters and less than
    complete fulfillment
we know we all face the same blank wall at about
    a quarter to four
       on a sad Saturday, with
children's voices playing outside, and the
    creak of ancient trees.

We all go through a dark door.

But if light doesn't shine from our faces
then the little paradoxes, as small as the
spots on an ant's underbelly, will have
    eclipsed us like the
great burning sun itself, we rolling

over like the sea, pure

light glittering on our crests.

1/6

HIT

With agile tomb and broken pencil bent
he scuffles as he crosses blasted pastures

and slips alongside shadows barely noticed
by the border guards of mental innocence,

for he is blastworthy, like a detonator, could
go up any second in spray or syncopation at best

as he plunders on trudging Coptic corridors
at marvelous slants up pyramidal angles.

He wrote this himself. Knew it was futile.
Parabolic catalogs hardly contain the multitudes.

Not that containment is quite required by law
in this cosmology, but peculiarities do accrue.

And the sky is full of dirigibles that darken it.
He's been hit. Not hard. But definitely

he's been hit.

1/7

ADDRESS

In memory of Imam Alphahim Jobe

I came across an address in my address book
of someone who has since died,
   written in his own hand.
His hand actually wrote his name, address and
  phone number with a blue ballpoint pen, in his
inimitable handwriting, funny "a's," peculiar
   "t's," all the idiosyncrasies of a
handwriting accrued from childish scrawl through
   High School stress and frenzy and
     college's incessant note-taking
to this little ballpoint plaque in my address book
of this man who was a real
Gambian prince of a man, who died
   mysteriously in the
     back seat of a New York taxi after
minor fender-bender,
and I thought of the space he existed in
to write this down in my book,
I thought of his heart and brain and
movements in this world and wondered at the
space or spacelessness he may
now be in, out of which, while alive,
he wrote his name and address, hand out of
   sleeve, holding the
pen just so, to

write it down.

HE WAVED GOODBYE

He waved goodbye as he flew off the
   side of the hill, he
had no need of wings or birdbrain, but
just took off running, flapping his arms

like we do in dreams. He
wasn't dreaming. Maybe the

cypress trees circling the black lake that
looked like silver in the sun
   were the ones dreaming, or the
too green hill itself that now was
blackboard to his running shadow as it
   rippled up bumps and down hilly indents,
maybe the city at its very base was
dreaming, heat ripples also making the great
classical domes and endless stairways insubstantial, but

he really couldn't bother working out which was
awake and which was asleep because
he was flying — he'd always

wanted to fly, he wanted to
always fly, to touch down only for the

earthly essentials, prayer that has to do with
kneeling and putting his
   head on the chopping block of the ground
and lovemaking, though if he could
do that flying too he'd be

satisfied. The song of his flight goes
something like the sound of about a
hundred well-oiled bicycles, that free
   clattery sound like parchment flapping,
and the words we could catch him singing just the
corners of like *"bugle," "dingle," "gong,"*
   "marsupial," strange

combos, but as he flew his own
distinctions faded as blue sky invaded him
more and more until his own

outlines and the area of conscious space

with its eyes trained in front of him
he inhabited and the entirety of the
whole sky became one singing entity, or
no single entity at all, more like a

disembodied humming, not too far
removed from that first instant when

God just said to the universe: Be!

SURROUNDED BY INCOMPREHENSION

Surrounded by incomprehension, surrounded by
incomprehension and beauty, bright
emerald green snake rising up in
   dark grass, crystal, raining continually
     down, hedged all around with

incomprehension and an unspeakable beauty of
each moment fitting perfectly into place like
intricate mosaic-work on a flat surface
   which this is not, it is
     wedged three dimensional

actions through space in
   one door out the other, intimately
     connected to our bodies and the
ocean tide breaths in and out our dangling
bodies depend on, consciousness unique to
   each of us and of each of us the same,

we face out from a single consciousness and face
a single consciousness before us,
circled as we are by incomprehension in the sense that
do we really comprehend what we see? (The
   muffled heartbeat responds), do
others comprehend *our* mysteries?
(Their heartbeats also boom.)

Ringed round with beauty that
circles like the ever-circling animals, trees and

rocks that longed to hear Orpheus' music and
so drew near — he sat on a
  rock and sang what was
     already outside him, all those
circumference beast ears just pricked
    up at the sound his
      own songs gave them, his own songs
sprouted ears, and all those many ears listened,

God singing to Himself through the magnificence that we
are, transparent as glass on a
  mountaintop of beauty that
glistens.

Listen.

1/9

ON THE THIN MAGISTERIAL BORDERLINE

On the thin magisterial borderline
   stand a million trillion beings
letting the radiant suns of both worlds
   land on their heads.
There stand Pegasus, the unicorn, the centaur,
   half real, half unreal, wings and a
      horn and a man's torso
         springing from the
      giant body of a horse,

or butterflies big as houses, who come to
   people in dreams, with old lovers' faces
      where normally the insect's
         faces would be,

flowers who sing in chorus, softly after midnight,
trying to woo distant stars and occasional planets,
and then the distant stars themselves whose silky
   voices spiral through space, through
endless black iciness to fall on the flowers' heads.

Things so utterly microscopic no human
   microscope can see them,
but perfectly formed and functional existing
   in perfectly normal dimensions,
like the perfectly formed feet of
newborn hamsters, perfectly formed claws
   with their perfectly formed fingernails,
and inside the veins and capillaries carry

   blood from their perfect hearts whose
     tiny valves and chambers work as
         perfectly as ours.

Collapse this down a few hundred magnifications even
   more minute, and God's
     perfection still holds, even though
no human eye can see it, flourishing and vibrating and
singing its song.

Or things too giant to comprehend,
maybe living in the fifth dimension,
we only see a shadow now and then, or only a
    portion of their body, the Bermuda
      Triangle, strange

   visions on mountaintops, strange
     things in water that go for
    centuries unexplained, whose
dimensions are simply too vast for our human
   preceptors to comprehend.

On the thin magisterial borderline
stand a million trillion beings
letting the radiant suns of both worlds
land on their heads.

                          1/11

BLUE DARKNESS

Moving through space
often I get the feeling I'm on an
   incredible adventure
as if about to step onto a
platform with state-of-the-art
   hydrogen balloons that
lift off and sail to a remote
      Himalayan village,

or, once in that village, I'm entering a
street under dark thatched roof that leads to
    a room with smiling face
hovering in its sepia depths who'll
show me the single silver-edged breath that
completes my transport of enlightened
    annihilation and beyond.

Then something in the everyday air, even my regular
   bodily movements across a room or out a
     familiar door, has intensity
direction and arrival at the magnificence of
   unexpected riches.

Other times, heart beating with its usual naïve bravado,
I go down stairs or out door, into car, into
   building, answer phone, with a

dull ache, a nagging recollection of such things as
heading out onto high seas with foreign

crew and blind captain, over gold and maroon
   waters, islands slowly emerging with their
dripping green fringe and plonging xylophones,

something in the air gives both weight and buoyancy,
connects to a youthful certainty that anything is possible
and *will* happen, we face out in a new direction, everything

falls into place in meaningfully unusual configurations,
something is being constructed in pure
   space I can then stand back from
      and see in its entirety, like a city from a hill,
each breathing having constructed it,
each eyeblink having added to its height,
each heartbeat having contributed to its

bright light burning deep there
in a hollow of blue darkness.

                                             1/12

SIGNS OF THE END

I look for signs of the end of time
   in the spillage of ink on a page
      and the shape it makes,
in the strange light out the window, glaring gray sheet
in front of
   unknown landscapes,

odd sounds of voices coming from adjoining rooms,
the way people rush into disaster with
   both eyes open, clutching at their
bodies in this world's shrinking cosmology,

honking sounds of geese passing invisibly in the
     sky above,
car crash sounds invisibly ahead of me
   on the highway below.

If I close my eyes, lids blotting out the world,
the end of time is near.
Clock dangling into a maelstrom.
Voice cracked at a high note,
earthquake in the heart as my heartbeat
   doubles a beat or skips a beat,
dead telephone receiver, anonymous
phone call after midnight with
   ominous click and then silence.

Stasis.

Everything coming suddenly or
    gradually to a stop.
My own toppling. My own falling

forward into a swarm of stars.

                                           1/13

SMALL BITS OF ADVICE

If you topple from a great height,
fall up.

If you sing in the night
make roses bloom.

If you dance with harlots
see their faces as jewels.

If you set fire to your life
speak to each flame as your brother.

If you leap over an abyss of darkness
wear a jacket of light.

If you sink below your usual elevation,
call the mermaids to welcome you.

If you lie down in the mud of shame,
feel the wheels of chariots roll over you.

If you go through the doorway of acceptance
wear no expression on your face

but your own.

In private laugh, in public weep.
Let your smile be the cloth of the desert.

Send all but the best away,
then lavish bounties and sweets.

Listen intently with both ears.
Sound is not of this world.

Speech is the saint in our bodies
calling us home.

                                                     1/14

SIMPLE QUESTIONS

Green boats float on the surface of the air,
butterflies fly in and land on the furniture,
a blue mist always surrounds the mountain,
agony lies in a string in loops on the tabletop,
   slightly buttered.

It's an old abandoned mansion on a thousand
     acres of land. She's been
dead a year and comes back often
  to survey the damage time
     wreaks with its
     insistent dripping.

She wears a wide hat and whistles aloud
    in the empty rooms.
I loved her then, though I may not love her now,
her phosphorescent bones.

She had eyes men would kill for. They
reflected back your life to you, made
    afraid turn to unafraid in
two minutes of simple questions:
"Tired?" "Been to the mountaintop?" "Ever
    killed anyone?" "Does your
heart hang in a golden cage suspended in a
turquoise sky above Raven's Crest Peak?"

You'd follow her with your eyes as she
    waltzed around the shadowy

    room singing lullabies. Her
hands making arabesques and pirouettes in
nowhere. She made

nowhere itself come alive by her presence.

Now she turns presence into nowhere when she
passes through rooms with her
   smile and icy chill. Her
restless future. The quick birds who
    fly through the rooms and
through her outline.
Ringtails and goshawks and finches flashing yellow
as they sail out the door.

Her name was Forever, but we
never knew what Forever really
   meant until she
vanished from our sight. Forever extended way out
   past her, and every time we
blink we look directly into it.

Shhh. Here she comes again.

I hold my heart in my hands.

                              1/15

DOWN A LONG SHADOWED ALLEYWAY

Down a long shadowed alleyway I
　long to go, say, in some
　　　interesting conveyance like
a body wholly peaceful with itself the way
　I imagine saints or Buddha or
Muhammad, peace be upon him, was, light
falling on his face at intervals that
chinks in the woven rattan
　　roof let in, passing

market tables filled with goods, extending a
hand, expressing a
　smile to a half-shadowed clerk in
　　mercantile obscurity,
down this alley, conveyed, toward a

monumental meeting, say, with a fabulous
beast with burning eyes I'd ask a question and
it'd lie, I'd know it lied, and
Tai Chi smooth as silk take out my
　sword and slice it clean in two
and as the halves fell away,
hey, a gorgeous maid appears,
steps out of dragon rubble, lifts
a moon-perfect face to me and actuality
shimmers, hard reality shivers into its

vibratory components, electric charges so
fast and busy they make this

spectacle we see, supercharged tiny
red and blue sparks running almost
invisibly through everything, alchemical
   gold fared forth in dimensional
     splendor to make beds and

tables and doorways and other
people, as well as
ourselves, conveyed in
more or less uncomfortable bodies,
never unlumpy or quite coordinated enough

to just stand still and blessedly be!

                                            1/16

FAIRY TALE

Once upon a time
there lived three princesses, Toil, Amnesty
   and Perturbation.

Toil was recognizably bedraggled, hair all
   snaggly, dress torn, face blotched and
      smudged, feet splayed. Poker
in hand. Nail in teeth.

Amnesty was fat, jolly, sunny, looked
  always on the bright side, thought
everyone would improve, flash of
  eye and sparkle of teeth, forgiving.

Perturbation was sallow-complexioned, slope-
   shouldered, skinny as a drawer-pull,
      quick tempered, darting of eye,
      rapid-fire of tongue, hysterical.

They set out one day to bring order out of chaos,
tame the savage breast, bridge the
  gap, cross the great divide,
generally cross all "t's" and dot all "i's."

They first met Stubborn Obstinate, a
   short, mean, miserly
      man with down-turn of nose and
         up-thrust of jaw and
bandy of leg and balloon of belly. He was no

frog you could kiss and have a prince,
nor was there any talking to him at all, for he
glared with yellow semaphore eyes and already
had all the retorts you'd expect for every
good word and kind suggestion.
Some folks are just made that way.

Enter a large cow.
A black cow with a dog's face.
Named Blight.
Blight bleated and barked and when you
milked her you got bricks. Thick bricks.
Which delighted Stubborn Obstinate whose
cow it was.

The three princesses wept copiously while
    putting on sweaters and raincoats
and buying tickets for the islands.
I'd go myself if I could, what with this
    crazy weather.
I wonder if I'd have any peace there.
And yet from the snake of concern
uncoils the yoke of human kindness.

The three princesses were frogs and felt
    better in ponds.

Me, I'm happiest in the
    tropics.

Except for the bugs.

THE SPARK

A big curvaceous cello, with sides so
  highly polished and burnished to a
    high sheen you can see your
      face in it, and the
faces of your loved ones. A big brass

gong, also brought along, to accompany my
  song, struck with felt
    mallet, soft but strong
sound resounding through all
    other sounds,

such as the high-pitched trumpet, uptight
  notes held at a great
    height, piercing but
bright, floating across all other
    sounds a few decibels
      above, like the
  surface of the
glittering sea above
    treacherous coral.

So the orchestra of the world convenes
each with its part to play,
and into this air of musical space
comes a spark, a flinch of light,
a pinched explosion of flame into a
  tiny conflagration, in which

say, the present-day eruption of Etna
    can be seen, the
ancient effluvia of Pompeii, the original
fire of man so closely guarded, even
    worshipped, the
fire in the belly,

but this spark

sails into open space and casts its light,
    held up on sound,
contains a universe or two, one

extruding from the other, where there was
none. A spark so

bright all dark
oceans could be illumined by it,
and fishermen trawl by its
light.

One spark!

1/19

HORSE

for Sahar von Schlegell in memory of her father

"Bring me my horse!"
"Father, you have no horse.
We sold it to pay for your funeral.
Besides, we couldn't get it up the
   stairs five flights."

"Then bring me my transistor radio."
"Father, that too is gone. We
  had to buy food for your
last days on earth. We had to buy
medicines."

*"The days are long, the winds are
   strong. My own father's
extending his hand. Through
traffic noise and rock'n'roll
my ancestors are extending
   their hands."*
"Father, the room is dark
and the gypsies have died.
Here's garlic and bright cloth,
here's a clock with its
hands torn off, and the
plastic melted."

*"Bring me the carton of snapshots.
I want to gaze at them*

*one last time, and
    say goodbye."*
"They too are gone, when the
    house burned down."

*"Then bring me my wife. I'll
look on her sweet face again."*
"Ah, dear father, she left us last year,
and waits on the other side of the
river for you, all dressed in
white, standing above black water."

*"Is there nothing at all to bring your father,
is the world so poor and I so poor
there's nothing at all to bring?"*
"We brought it all, and it was
nothing. All webs, and cobwebs,
entangled in webs. What you want now,
    father, is untangled
and free."

*"Then bring me your faces, one by one, to
    kiss goodbye."*
"Here, dear father, is a forehead,
here a warm cheek. Your lips are
    cold, father, the room is dark."

*"Bring me my horse. With the golden
    saddle. I will
ride it now."*

"Here's your horse, dear father.

Here's your horse."

1/20

PAST MIDNIGHT

As I turn the light out
and lie down
I feel an enormous planet
   turning at a tilt inside me,
revolving in a sea of debris backlit with stars,
   blue-gray mist twinkling in space,

then I get up to write it
down and it's gone. I so wanted to write

constellations of crystal roses,
something breathtaking, each rose the
size of Saturn, each one revolving,

that we don't have to go anywhere to
explore the universe, just let it

open up inside an indefinite dimension I'm
convinced is literally out of
time and space, flying

alligators as well as entire floating
islands each with groves of
flowering orange trees, people passing and
   pausing down the
petal-strewn lanes between them,

and glimpsed far above and only God knows how
far away, a constant play of

vivid rainbows revolving against
   velvet black, impossible
to describe, leaping arcs of the bent spectrum from
light's invisibility to the

visibility of all the colors
at work or at rest in this now
lamplit room around me as I

write down what was just a
passing momentary experience, but

was urgently anti-gravitational enough to
get me out of my soft bed past midnight

to sit up and write it down.

                                                        1/21

SOAP THE BUTTON

Soap the button, grab the fox,
   dip the dog in castor oil,
blow the window full of air,
   dig your fingers in the soil.

Look for luck, kiss a frog,
   sing your heart out, say your prayers,
thumb a ride and whistle Dixie,
   make a mess of your affairs.

I love Paris, hate Tahiti,
   live to slurp the foam off top,
sing some loathsome low graffiti,
   kiss the closest traffic cop.

If you're living on the edge,
   shining light to desperados,
don't forget to carry sledge
   to hammer down the avocados.

Hunt for red October, smile,
   you're eternally on Candid Camera,
sing an aria from Puccini,
   ride to heaven on zucchini,

wear the homburg not the beanie,
   disappear with abracadabra,
I love Lucy, so do you,
   everything is flying high,

pet the cat, don't touch the cougar,
  push away with Captain Bligh,
if you've lasted on earth this long
  not like flies that die on Tuesday,

maybe something wonderful's happening,
  a stand-inside-your-very-own-shoes day.

1/21-22

FROM THE PEAK

From the peak you can see
in all directions at once.

The eye is an agate
in a crystal cup.

The eye in the clouds that
blinkless looks back
is symbolic.

I see valleys in the distance,
hamlets, towns.

Way in the distance
old boats in the sea, surrounded by
    dragons.

A feel of heaven
close on the cheek.

A sensation of light
on the lips.

At certain altitudes
your hair becomes the wind.

Your heart becomes the mind
and thinks the whole universe up.

But it's only a reflection, a
distorting mirror on fire.

Love that fire like doves
flying out of the woods.

In the distance we remain
as indelible as ever.

1/23

WE BLINK

If you stay aloft in an airplane after the air's
    gone out,
or take a walk on the earth after the
    earth's dissolved,
go swimming off Jamaica when all the water's
    gone south,
apocalyptically,

take a breath after death's found you out,
after death's refrigerator door's closed on you yet you
sit up and dare to breathe, to bat your
    eyes
(Orpheus did something like this, head
continued to sing floating down the Nile,
    Osiris, beautiful melodies out of
        dead lips),

the eyes look on other sights, maybe in
    silhouette *(ah, my dear*
we'll never be apart though teams of
caparisoned elephants come between, between
    one state of consciousness and the
        next),

we blink and cherry trees blossom with
    darting birds,

we blink and it's a ship going down nose
    first, the Titanic, unsinkable,

  as if made of balsa,

we blink and desert sand blows across the screen
where not long before tropical fruits and
  flowers burst into
   pure rainbow colors to nearly
    blind the eye,

we blink and we're babies,
blink again on adolescent angst in sudden
  twists of fate,
then open our eyes and we're
dead. The world's wheels
  grinding overhead.

Way down below, in cool salons,
deep harpsichord music serenades the
  dreamers floating like
 algae on the
   surface of a pond.

The whole world blinks in exact
  syncopation with our
   lids.

God bless us in the evening
when the sun goes down.

            1/24

THE DJINN IN THE BOX

Wee Willie Winkie bought a painted box
and when he got home he opened it and a djinn came out.
"*Command!*" he boomed, his
    head past the roof looking
down at Willie through clouds.
A strapping purple djinn with his big arms crossed.
Satin jacket, satin pants, the whole nine yards.
Wee Willie yelled

*"Get me outta my mortality, I
never do the right thing, don't
know which way to go
or how hard to push! The whole
world's charade is played in a house of cards –
I wanna be free!"*

The djinn's face softened. He expected
stretch limousines, Frank Lloyd Wright chalets on rocks,
full roomfuls of riches.
He leaned down real close, big moon face
    next to Willie's.
"*Look here,*" he said, turning his perfectly round head,
and the sky gave way to chambers,
rooms bursting with light,
figures coming and going, carrying

    flower-shaped radiances, incandescent escalators,
shedding phosphorescences of light, blue
entrances through light,

    corners onto open fields, walls collapsing onto
yellow prairies of song, elegant
heartbeat music, doors of green mist,
horses whiter than crystal lifting into the air,
silver fountains of sweet drink, gorgeous faces at
    distant windows, then

down through the layers to Willie, wide-eyed,
his own heartbeat satisfied.

"I'll take you there whenever you want, Willie,"
the turning moon face said, huge lids lowering
    over giant eyes.

Willie lowered his head.

There's no record of what he said.

                                                                           1/26

DICTATION

A tall figure comes into the room
(he's a lot taller than an
   African basketball player),
he has the head of a woman on him, and he's
   carrying a tablet, blank at the
moment, a thin red mist
    floating above it, but I can
see words starting to
sort of chisel themselves
      out on it –

his quill, which he holds in his
   right hand, is
     bigger than a redwood,
his smile, playing across his
   face, is longer than the Nile.

He does a shuffle. He's
   always in motion.
His eyes, with those extra-long
    lashes, dart to and fro, not out of
  nervous expectation, but rather so as
not to miss anything. They're
kind and cheerful eyes, black as
   coal against snow-white
     sclera.

He has a voice – it's like a loudspeaker in a
   stadium, far away and

    loud at the same time,
and he
commands me to write
  the words being
    chiseled on the
tablet, which are the

words I write in my notebook before the
tide of human traffic flows through as if I were

just another guy standing on the
    sidewalk in the

way of Progress.

1/27

ONE DAY

Suddenly giant cubes started filling up the
horizon. Unprecedented.
Closets started filling up with feathers.

Refrigerators had voices. (Open the door: *voices.*
   Close the door: *silence.*)
Turn on a light switch
and the room started to rain.

Moustaches grew on children. Long, bushy
Gold Rush type moustaches.
And it was on any nonchalant day, nothing
   abnormal, swans gliding
in the sky, automobiles
     driven by ferrets.

Telephone operators giddily spoke Yiddish,
cockroaches wore little military uniforms
and could be heard muttering orders
     under their breath.

Light bulbs were filled with flakes.
And I had come home early.

I opened the door onto a
   redwood forest.

Well, I walked right in, down a
thick, needle-carpeted lane

where golden sunlight glinted between
giant shadows, and I
leaned for a moment against
the friendliest, warmest, shaggiest most
    hospitable bark in the world.

(Something about living in a redwood forest
    soothes the soul.)

Did I mention the sound the creek makes as its
    water curls across rocks?

Pure melody!

                                                1/27

THE TRUTH IS REVEALED

In a harsh, uninviting climate
where the earth is so cold it gets hard as bone
  and the air almost dangerous,

in a place ringed with active volcanoes
    extending their plumes,
behind great tumble falls of rock, where
    mountainsides can give way any
      second, the roar of their
crash like a pin dropping
down through an abyss in the night in the
total scheme of things,

in an exchange of well-sealed test tubes
between two orbiting astronauts high above
    the Himalayas,

in an almost imperceptible signal between
    two snorkelers idling among pink coral,
on a windy day in Chicago, the sky
    like a cauliflower of clouds,

the truth is revealed.

It doesn't fall in flakes or snake around
    corners, it doesn't
      wait for the elements to
crack open or
the water to run out,

it displays itself openly without fuss or bother
like a beam of sunlight hitting the chilled sides of a

water glass to a person who
hasn't had anything to drink for
days, silent

as rock.

1/31

IN-BREATH OUT-BREATH

Lakes, clear, lazy, lying
  off in the distance,
roof-slopes in curves against bright blue sky,
mountains, echoes of mountains
    almost as blue as the sky,
flurry of lights in the air, crisp as crystals,
  showers of crystals
    scintillating the air,
cold clear air
we draw into our bodies lung-first, mixed
  in the blood and
    distributed, sent to the
outlying districts, light in the darkness,
pumped up corpuscles, inflated, happy,
to finger and toe-tips, we
  stretch as we
stand against this alpine landscape,
    Switzerland of the
      mind maybe, altitudinous,
before descending on the
outbreath to lagoon-filled tropical
  clamminess and heat, large
    leaves clustering, black
water top, lotuses, distant
  xylophone music, lapping sounds,
    fly-buzz, mosquito-
      buzz, hibiscus.
The outbreath of carbon dioxide,
deflated corpuscles

```
      waiting the élan of pure
          air again, droopy,
      expecting excitement, a fresh
          cold slap in the
              face of drowsiness, the putt-putt of

      outboard motorboat across black lagoon
      replaced by scrunch-sound of blue

      white snow as we
      prepare to descend.
```

THE TOWER IN THE LAKE

We traveled down to the tower
but it was below the water level,

the place rumored to have been
where they saw the handprint of God.

It was a wide day. The three of us together,
Maj, the humped dumpling, the Green Sage

and I.
We traveled silently.

When we arrived, we could see only the
top of the tower down in the water, and the

sun above our heads down in the water,
and the three of us together peering

down into the water.
"There is an entranceway, even to the Unseen, by

a nature aperture," said the Green Sage.
Something we'd expect him to say,

he with whom we always feel completed.
Maj winked and whistled, plopped

rocks into the water, scuffled.
"All this way for nothing!"

"But the nothing was why we came," I replied,
hoping I was right. I glanced

hoping to see approval in the
Green Sage's eye, but he stayed in profile.

Presently the water subsided.
Various eel-like things slithered away.

A clear ringing sound began in the sky.
The tower seemed to rise from the water.

I patted the water onto my face for protection.
It's true that the day's revealed to us

its treasures. Her
onyx leaves, her gliding streams, her

rough roads.
If I hadn't seen it myself I'd

never have believed it.
For inside the tower was another lake

and inside the lake another tower.
And we were identical.

And the handprint of God was everywhere.

HOME FOR THE OWL

Home for the owl is a high tree bough,
home for a mouse is a deep-down hole,
home for man is his hopes and his fears
but his deepest home is Allah.

Honeybees store their pollen in hives,
spiders store their food in webs,
man holds everything close to his heart
but his deepest heart is Allah.

If a bird flies far it knows its way home,
salmon fight fierce rapids upstream,
when we leave on a trip we know its end
but its true end is always Allah.

We end where we began, in the middle of the world,
in the center of our universe of love and pain,
we never venture far from the center of our being
but its center is only Allah.

GAMES

We'd enter by the main gate
without the need of key
and hang around inspecting
stones and names till half past three.

We'd read the names and float along
and some would creep behind
and pounce and scare the others
screaming *"Seek and ye shall find!"*

The night was dark and dense and deep,
our games were merry play,
I long for them just as I long
for those who could not stay.

It's funny how you choose your friends:
we'd all been hit by cars.
We'd come together, smile, and then
show off our gruesome scars.

But now I float around alone
wondering what it was I'd done,
to interrupt my life that way,
when I was twenty one.

I guess I'll never know for sure.
I sink back in the ground
as this sad planet rolls around
and around and around.

DRIVING IN SILENCE

I wonder how many people drive in their cars,
   if they're alone,
in complete silence?

No rock'n'roll, no Brahms symphony, no
   daily news.
Silence. The small motions of right foot on
   gas pedal, shifted over onto
     brake, steering ever-so-slightly
in a vast and fast-moving metallic lozenge
going past landscapes

with no sound inside the car but the thoughts in your
   head and their whispery dissipation,
your heartbeats' syncopated *oompah* with every
spring-creak and road-bump as the
car flows along.

The great chamber of the heart beating as thoughts above
come and go in their whiskery nimbus.

Mental islands of particulars bobbing and
disintegrating into the surrounding sea.

Eyes focused always forward, until it seems
the whole car lifts up and skims along at an
   elevated altitude, head
pressing against clouds, a little swerve
     to the right, big blur of

> things and people and
> trees and other
> cars as they
> noisily pass by,

filled with stereophonic distractions, or
inhabited by other human beings

also dwelling for a time in

complete silence.

2/6

CHECKLIST

A blue locomotive that goes nowhere, a
   porcelain cuckoo in a cage that
     tweets Mozart, three
glass pianos end to end painted bright red,
a mysterious room behind black drapery no one
    goes into,
cars of all vintages and various leopard upholsteries,
office furniture with gliding contours made of
    tubular aluminum,
clocks out of polished mahogany in the shape of
famous Disney characters,
   stickers from foreign countries to put on the
     sides of leather steamer trunks,
autobiographical treks into darkest Africa
    or brightest Mongolia,
books in Swedish with lithographic plates
   showing exotic plants and the
    organs of the human body on
     transparent cellophane flaps,
several bullets of differing calibers,
several packets of love letters from
   several deceased admirers,
stuffed bugs in glass cases with neon markings
   and wings like isinglass,
flip books that animate a juggler standing on his
   head while juggling a bicycle, a torch,
    the Eiffel Tower, Ethel Merman,
bars of light like gold bullion stacked
   to the ceiling in an abandoned

railroad station,
brochures from Indochina describing the
    pleasures of tourism before 1920,
several working telephones in the shapes of
    movie stars from the silent era,
I don't know how many certificates of
    authenticity about things that are
        now broken,
voice recordings from famous heads of state
    abdicating all responsibility for the
    irreparable damage they've caused,
letters of farewell from European circus
clowns who've met their
    true loves in the last
        city they visited,

mounds of sand dunes, some disguising
    unexcavated pyramids,
acres of butterfly reserves where gazelle roam
    chewing the leaves off shrubs,

these and a billion other things on lists kept in
lacquered chests from the Ming Dynasty,
are what I will leave behind when I

finally put off gloom's clothing and enter
a suit of total bewilderment to board

ecstasy's time machine for making the
    transworld trip to planets only
        seen in dream among

couches of live animals who all have
faces of angels in spotlit
   lights of pure gold,
and I pray it happen to everyone before it's
too late or too unimportant,

that we enter the natural state of joy
God gave us in the first place so we might
recognize our good fortune in stepping

foot on the planet before leaving it entirely
to go where it is we were really created for

before the clock strikes midnight on a dark
street in a tall black house down a long
   corridor last
week in Vienna during a
   thunderstorm with a
     white horse waiting for us
by a lamppost

whose collar has our name on it
but who answers to the sound of silence

and so takes off without us
down the Street of No Return.

We wave to ourselves from opposite windows!

We sink into ourselves
just glad to be alive!

THE FACE OF GOD DIRECT

If a man could be at ease with an
  avalanche that's
    taking away his house and family,
sit and converse with it, ask it its name and
just how it's feeling, where it
  plans to go from here, or

a woman be on speaking terms with a
flash flood that's sweeping away her
    belongings in
  billows of brown froth,
a grandpa have a chat with lightning:
*"Where do you come from? How do you
  like it here? Will you be
    staying long?"*

Or newlyweds really get to know a
house fire, be on a first-name basis with its
   incandescent core as it
   runs its hands up the
new curtains and in a single *whoosh*
    cleans out the closet.

If the intern in white gown and loosely tied
  cap and face-mask could
speak the language of plague, share
reminiscences with an ancient virus,
discuss the Middle Ages and the works of Rabelais,

if the drowning boy could sing the song of his
drowning, sing close
   harmony with the forces that are
      sucking him down,

then we'd all get closer to the radiant
brilliance of our lives and see the
clean-shaven face of death with its
   dreary eyes and mouth of
      sweet deceiver, its bald head and
high cheekbones, its glittering
         intentions,

sit on an edge where only squirrels
perch, talk freely about

the long river voyage, the hair-thin bridge-crossing, the
twelve moons oscillating slowly against the
low black ceiling of the sky,
the tree of wisdom as fragile as egg shell
and as strong as a high waterfall
plunging through all the worlds to a
   depth of a billion miles,

our names being played back to us
by glassy mountain passes and
churning valley river waters beyond.

If only the inside of our skins and the
outside of the inner parts of everything
could communicate freely, soul and

   body intertwined, water and
rock, bark and heart of tree opening leafy arms,
taking everything in and letting
  everything out again, a
loose hold on the
things of this world, a tight
    grip on the
  things of the next,

we'd all be sitting in the multiple bodies of light
we know are our natural habitats,
in a warm breeze, this side of the
forest of recognition, bathing in its
        radiance.

Then we might see the Face of God direct.

"Hello parking ticket, serious gash from a
sharp object, death of a loved one,
daily aches and pains and psychological agony,
sexual torment, fear of mortality...
been here long? Any plans for after?
Thoughts for the future? What are your
deepest desires?

I'm Abd al-Hayy.
Been on the planet 57 years,
trying to sing
one true song.

You?"

NOVEL

I would like, as in so many works of literature,
to begin by describing my protagonist. He's
listless, yet restless, talented yet limited,
he wears corduroy pants, large twill, and
loose shirts open at the collar. He had gone to
school until he grew bored with it,
he traveled, wrote, visited famous people, asking
    pertinent questions, getting
        personal answers, yet
making no use of them.

In an earlier age, he would be described as a
dilettante, even a dandy. Smart, too smart,
sociable yet withdrawn, garrulous yet
    mysterious, and never running out of
money, with no apparent source, I see him

leaning on a boat rail, an ocean liner, his
blond hair battered by the wind, like
    golden flags, his sharp features
        reddened by the sun,
he squints and smiles, leans his head back,
laughs.

He hears hippopotamus in his mind. The
    flap of pages of Herodotus. Original
        parchment editions. In drafty
Austrian library rooms, echoes of
    chair legs against hard wood, screech of

    gulls.

He's back by the railing watching dolphins.

The ring he's wearing belonged to the Countess.
I wonder where he's stashed his diary? I'd
love to see the entry for December 12th.
Was he the owner of the shadow cast across
    the Duberstrasse? Did his
laughter echo on the rock walls of the midnight street?

I'd like to introduce my protagonist and
follow him for a hundred pages or so, watch him
eat, make love to lanky women, wear
    expensive shirts, make some
deep contribution to literature or society.
His love of cold compresses, his taste for
    salmon. His dishonor. His
redemption. But

everything in fiction passes so fast, a
    whole life wound up and run down in
so few pages. Book closed. Casket cover
    sealed. Coffin lowered. We

hardly knew him. His name was
Roland. He dreamed of cats. Hundreds of wild
cats. Became tigers. Faces like moons.
Lions bounding across boundaries. Leaping
    lions with bodies
        elongated. Graceful. Leaping and

leaping. As if into fire. His last thoughts made him a lion. He

looked like a lion as he lay there, mane of white pillow around him. Beam of

light on his head.

A lion dying.

Then, a lion dead.

2/17

TEACHERS AND THE TEACHING

1

The blue desert sands stretch out in all
    directions. A little
forenoon is pushed onto the flat part
in a yellow wheelbarrow with black wheels.
I have sat in the circle, and now the
    ants come to me for counsel.
They carry leaves and small objects which they
    lay at my feet. I have so

little to say to them that will help them in their
quest for the perfect life. *"Work together.*
    Build well. Prosper and propagate."
What else can I say?
They are not disappointed. *"We are ants. You are*
    not. Your wisdom is your
        perspective."
They file away, touching feelers with the
latecomers to tell them what was
    said. The newer visitors just come
to take a look. I continue to
smile down at them. They deserved my
full attention, and I
    gave it to them.

The sun beats down. The day is long.
I look out across the wastes
    as the last ant disappears.

A dusky sun, pale brown, descends into the
sea of night through the bounding ocean of the sand's horizon.
I am also an ant. And

bow before One greater than I, asking for
   news.

2

I've tried to teach the young Count to play
   the harpsichord.
He always brings his vicious Pekinese with its
   dreadful red bow and
      rows of pointed teeth.

His mother sits with straight back in her
   miles of vermillion taffeta and
      taps time with her fan.
But little Frederick is abominable.
His hands are like rubber balls, always
   making fists. I can't get him to
spread his fingers on the keys.
Of course his ineptitudes are all my fault.

As he hammers relentlessly I
   gaze out at the symmetrically clipped
     hedges, the easy green openness so
restful to my eyes, my head, my heart.

Lesson over, they stand up, the dog

growls, they whisk away. Milady always says
"He's much improved!"
I wrench a smile and tilt my head to make it
more sincere. Downward, so she'll not
see me. Sneer.

Tomorrow they'll be back. Rain or shine,
as I'm the music master.
I live in a cold room.
I compose on a spinet.
I take my supper at seven.
I have seen a volcano light up the night sky.
I have nearly run aground on the high seas.
I've been to America, and played for a
    president.
All my relatives are dead.
My true love has also been lowered into her grave.
They'll be back tomorrow.
With the dog. Yellow eyes. White teeth.
Red bow. *With that*
devil incarnate of a
    dog!

3

The gold that is not called gold
    is true gold.
God Who is God is called upon as God.
The woods ring with His Name.
Leaves flutter to the ground, called

    groundward, all in
        God's audible Name
resounding through each atom, through tree-limb and
    ground and the good or bad
air in between.
Ducks round and round on the pond.
Sound as well as no sound.
The Name sounded and the Name unsounded.

And as fate would have it, we
    know that Name, we've been
taught that Name to call Him with, He's
given us His Name. And
nothing's ever been the same.
How light the air is, sweet and true!
We draw it in.
How little we know who we are or
    what we do.

And yet we're meant to know.
We are not the stones on the road.
We're the road.

And God is God.
The curtain falls back into place.
And hushed the voice.
An ant walks across.
No expression on its face.

There is a Face suspended before our face.
And light in space.

                2/18-19

LOOKING FOR SIGNS

Celestina MacNamara sat on her porch and
   stewed. She'd
seen a sparrow fall out of the sky
but the world marched on.
She'd read it as a sign, and that the

cornfield was in flames, the fences had wings,
Joe Barker's milk cow opened her mouth and
   sang opera, all these things
in Celestina's eyes constituted a
clear-cut map to apocalyptic destruction.
She already saw people in those
   wrenched gestures of the
survivors of Pompeii, including the
curled-up Labrador retriever, tongue
     lolling.

Then a distant barn door opened
and out trooped giant angels dressed in
     pure sky blue.
They flowed up to Celestina and formed a line.
She stood up and went down the
   row like a military dictator.
The face of one was visual honey.
Another's fresh as a farm boy, cherry-cheeked and
   raspberry-lipped.
Another like a sky full of fleecy clouds, blindingly
     white,
another as exotic as carved mahogany, polished to a

   smooth black sheen,
      eyes so coal-like, so burning, more
alive than any eyes she'd
   seen on earth in her short life.
And when she
came to the end of the line, they
   floated up in the air and
      disappeared, comforting

Celestina as much by their
disappearance as by their initial appearance.

But now the hills looked empty.
The noon shone in the remaining air, with its
   glare-light.

The day hung loosely around the trees and buildings, but
she heard a
soft melodious sound that was actual
   song-sound behind the
sounds that reached her ear.

Car horn. Song. Door slam. Song.
Human cry in the distance also
sounded like song. Tractor in the

distance. Song. And now
the world revolved around

inside that song.

                                              2/22

PERPETUAL MOTION

Perpetual motion was a concept that intrigued
small person Helwig.

All day he contemplated not only its
possibility but its actuality.

Walking along in his small person body
dwarfed next to giant machinery, full grown
   pines, soaring mountains,
small person Helwig tuned his interior to the
slowest setting so he could see the
workings of the universe as they were happening.
Instead of just seeing sky and underneath it water,
small person Helwig saw
water rising in nearly invisible droplet veils from
rushing creeks, glinting iridescently in the
light, silkily bending and straightening as it
rises into the glorious heavens, there to
coagulate, condense, then
cascade down as rain so those
homesick drops (everything's homesick)
can nestle back in their creek beds to go
careening seaward.

Small person Helwig saw big luminous
circles in the air, traced them with his forefinger,
the perpetual motion of water up in its
   arc and down in its shower.
His little eyes went level, he saw

    energy going like elfin lanterns from
moving thing to thing, he saw
emotional energy being transferred more or less
    unconsciously from person to person
and smiled at the plain sunny landscape of it all,
the open movements so obvious to his
observations, then he saw

wheels, motor wheels with connecting belts that
made other wheels turn,
wheels of cars and buses and wildly jerking
    taxicabs whose goose-honks
        startled him,
wheels of light also catapulting through space
illuminating as they go, lighting up

storefronts, arenas, faces, fingertips,

things dancing in each other's circumferences,
    tossing their hair,
things rising into the air on their
circumferential momentums,
    then back to water, great
wheels of waterfalls, water rotating
    down blank mountainsides into
pools,

then the oceans themselves like great rotating
wheels turning perpetually out past each
    continental edge
under the sun's preponderance, in the endless

lunar glow of inner contemplation.

Small person Helwig remembered his birth
and saw his death coming, flat wheel
entering from behind him and
making its exit somewhere up ahead,

oceanic plunge into life and out of it again,
and at the far end up ahead

entering the ocean of no return whose
great wheel still manages to

bring all things round again, like a
single song.

2/23

DOWN INTO THE POOL

Down into the pool we threw the
   lamp and the green bicycle.
We saw them sail slowly down.
They hit the black water and
   slid through with a splash.
We saw our faces and the sky.
We heard the slowly dripping water.

Next we threw down the bureaus.
Photo albums of twenty generations of
    Romanians, three of Bohemians.
Then we threw down the whole house.
Nothing was too big or too cumbersome.

Of course nothing was thrown down into the
   pool but a few pebbles.

Then we threw in a car, a building, an
    elevator, a hat pin, a toothbrush
      reportedly used by Abe Lincoln,
and numerous personal articles dear to
both of us. Of course

nothing was really thrown down into the pool,
although we threw our voices down a few times
saying smart things like *"Hello down there!"*
the listening to the echoes.

Then we got really ambitious. We

grabbed the night sky and threw it in.
All that extreme and bewildering darkness,
we threw it in. And evil. We

really wanted to throw in evil. Badness.
Man's inhumanity to man. Bloodthirstiness.
Power-mad stinginess and utter cruelty.
Government sanctioned torture and injustice.
We really wanted to throw that in.

Plus a plaster statuette of Laurel and Hardy.
A moonscape photo. A vial of blue liquid.
Spit.

But, of course, we didn't throw anything into the
   pool. We didn't even
spit into the pool.

We peered down into the darkness, heard the
eerie dripping, saw our faces rippling with
sunlit blue sky behind them,
bright sunlight making the
dark reflections of our faces even darker.

But we didn't throw anything
   down into the pool.

We only peered down at our faces.

We never threw anything down into the pool.

2/26

RACHEL, MAGDALENE, CELESTE AND BROOKER

Rachel, Magdalene, Celeste and
   Brooker walked along the green hillside
     with the sun in their faces.
Rachel, Magdalene and Celeste had appropriately
Biblical and celestial names, while
   Brooker stood out as being more
      earthbound, or at least
didn't carry the freight of such transcendent possibilities.

Now, Brooker was quite the mystic, obvious by
looking in her eyes, great
   wonders to behold, such as
     undersea landscapes, surfaces of
   distant moons of far-flung planets off of which
blew continual plumes of dust, sideways, into
the great vacuum of space.

Rachel, Magdalene and Celeste, moreover,
carried large hamburgers in their hampers,
waiting eagerly to flop on the hillside, giggling
    at some silly crack, and
   drag out their lunches and begin
     munching. They all had impeccable teeth.
They also all looked down on Brooker as being
     generally insufficient.

So, imagine their surprise, when they did finally flop,
when out of the sky came a large luminous
chunk of that sky, surrounded Brooker with its

    jaggedly zapping rays and
        excrescences of
  sharp, bright bolts of light,
and lifted Brooker bodily off that hill,
    her dainty hands dropping the
tiny cucumber sandwiches she had
made for herself, and the thinly sliced
      sweet pickle, dropped all these to

sail over the hill in a rainbow nimbus
off across the expanse, above a stand of
    cypresses and a meandering
river and way off past the
city nestled around Ararak Mountain,

for she had, by supreme command,
greater fish to fry and a spectacular
meeting prearranged for her, prearranged
centuries earlier, prearranged in eternity, and

Rachel, Magdalene and Celeste could only
look at each other and
wonder, going back to their
    munching.

Yes. Wonder.

Exceedingly.

2/26

FIGURES OF SPEECH

Whether the grain goes lengthwise or
   crosswise, we either go
with it or against it.

Whether waves pull us out or
   push us in we either
sink or swim.

If it's a clear day or if it's a bleak one
we either see forever or hardly at all.

It's not how many birds are in the bush
or if one's in the hand,
it's not if it's the school of soft knuckle-rolls

or the school of hard knocks,
if you've been only a few yards down the road or
all the way around the block,

it's really an alphabet soup where each
passing moment spells out headlines or
   obituaries,

celebrates the living or
sorrows the passing of the dead, with whom we may
   count ourselves
if we're not quick, and will be with soon
quick or no, so quickly do we

deathward go.

Yet not only is there

light at the end of the tunnel, there's also
tunnel at the end of the light,

and in that space we navigate
by Grace the circumambulating

globe.

2/27

THE FEELING OF WELCOME

In select locations on earth, in the
moisture of an eyelid, in the

shadow of a slender rainforest orchid after
the rains have stopped and strong golden

sunlight comes down,

in the tiny spaces between baby mouse paws,
in sexual heat at flex and bending points,

slippery sensations leading to dam-burst,
a scattering of white moths in the dark of night,

a constant rumble as currents flow
through the underwater hull of a treasure-laden shipwreck,

in the neural dot-dash patterns in the brain as
inspiration opens actual vistas where

before there were none, glades and
chasms, cliffs and brightly lit canyons,

lamplight in a bridal chamber,
voice of a child after a successful operation

coming out of deep sleep,

sound of parachute ropes extending as the

wind whistles past the

jumper only a few thousand feet above ground,

the licking of the letter flap as the lover says
goodbye to her beloved,

nothing needs to be said about them,
they need no odes or songs,

these moments in select locations on earth,
cheers from a stadium, the

front door opening and the return of the
long lost traveler after long absence,

a crystal that falls from the
hand onto a green velvet mat

and comes to rest upright, making a thousand
light-gleams spew out in perfect

star patterns.

Ducks finding their way home through stormy skies
a year later.

The central heart's imperviousness
to pain.

The feeling of welcome.

3/2

FORTUNE COOKIE

You will embark on a perilous journey.

You will not bump into the furniture on your
way out.

You will carry extra lightbulbs.

You will enjoy greater sexual horizons.

The plaintive cries of underground
creatures in distress
will affect your heart.

You will hear a movement in the walls.

You will interpret the chance juxtapositions of
clouds, and rather than
epic proclamations, you will speak
three poignant words: *"little bluejays tremble,"*
five words of admonishment: *"Ripe dogs kill
rambunctious squirrels,"* four words of warning:
"Beware the frozen bridge."

Con artists will try unsuccessfully to con you
though you may end up buying unwanted
real estate.

You will find yourself among prominent people.

Keep a low profile. Keep no
profile at all. *Get
rid of that nose.*

You will see the world as the
outer shell of an inner emptiness.

You're only looking at yourself. It's a
Catch 22. You should see how

the world sees *you!*

3/3

IN THESE BODIES

1

To meet in our bodies, to
  be of some use, to love,
to meet flesh to flesh, since in this world

we can't protoplasmically entertain collision and
maintain soul. The

hand that moves the plow also itches the
head, rubs the heart, the back, between
the beloved's legs,

smoothes out all rough spots, renews
tired tissue and aching limbs,

we are not cloud to scuttle the sea floor of air,
our memories are visceral, even

decades later we recall the smell and sound of it,
some fall, slight, yelling fit, amorous
foreplay, arch-backed consummation, as if

etched in bone, DNA recorded, infinitely
  play-backable, sunlight

on the cheek or
utter dark, cold or hot,

we cannot simply roll into each other, nor can we
unroll forever on our own and stay sane,
looking for love.
Inside this body of ours, male or
  female,
looking for the love flush, flash

of love light with full
Technicolor hurt or heartiness,

so familiar first experienced, so
indelibly a part of our flesh
thenceforward.

2

This body, like
antlers on a wall, like a
  pain in the middle of the night, like a
familiar but unknown voice heard through the
receiver of a telephone, like
the first rose on the bush, like a
cloud of dust that gets in the nostrils,

this body, like nothing else, sensations absolutely
our own and no one else's, how are we to
know? Dancing thigh muscles, arching
back, eyes darting to their corners to see
behind us at what is or
is not there,

we are spatial, encased in space. We are
space that sees and hears. Articulate
space. With
painful extremities, subject to
gravity's laws, and
the laws of the grave.

This body like dying, like coming back to life with a
snap of the eyelids hello,

this body like a fleshy old woman chasing a
youth through bushes to a beach, like a
finger-cracked old fisherman alone in moonlight,
  lingering over his line, looking
down, plops all
     around him,
hears them, sees them, but can't catch them,

this body ours but always elusive, we finally
die in it as if
strapped in a ritual canoe, and in so

doing are released from it, flying
out of it for good.

This body like a fragrant bar of soap,
like a flock of geese going south, the
  flap of their unison wings, one

sky, one light on their backs, one
warmth in their hearts, one

wisdom in their souls.

This body, given us on loan, returned to the
sea from which it came.

Lovely thing.

3

I think I shall die on a
night when there's no moon, though I should
like to die in pure moonlight,
ebb out to the edges of its scintillant whiteness.

I should like to die near a herd of deer,
in a place with flowers, near negro tombs.

Their songs.
Let the light in. I shall sing.

Let the cock rise and
crow. I shall not go now.

But one night will be the night before I die.
One day the day. What year will be the

year before this worn down body dies? Is this
passing moment, hand clutching pen, on a
longitudinal map to that
sudden stopping point?

Alas, open mouth, alas, open mind, flooded.
Open heart. Prairies getting light. Pearly

dawn light flowing forward toward the
awaiting hand that raises all this

as a conductor raises all the instruments to
hands and lips to begin a tone.

I'm sitting in my mummy now, consciously
thinking. God knows

I'm thinking.

3/4

IN A POEM

In a poem I like the spaces between the lines.

You can peer down between them at
    real things. A poem

shouldn't get in the way of real things. Lean

over, listen to the river cascading over rocks at the bottom,
light hitting water. Almost blinding
    glints.

The lines of a poem might be about flying
accordions, fences putting their
foot down, horses who
    walk right up to you with those
        leathery lips to ask for
directions. But if you

lean over a little and peer
down between the lines, the space that
opens up where before there was none, or
    none you could perceive,
you see real vistas, green mountains, valleys
all the way to the town in the

distance with blinking electric towers and
rapid transit systems, or you might see

tourmaline and zircon, gems tumbled on black

velvet, colors so naturally bright you
can't quite believe them, they're
too cartoon. The poem

frames them. They might not even be
mentioned, the poem might be about nightmares or
taking a walk in the park. But

between the lines are real
dragons with lashing tails,
real iron bridges over iron-black water,
real faces coming into close focus, their
eyes expressive and lips vulnerable, words

slow in coming. But
between the lines is a romantic affair that works,
a loyal lover in a

sky filled with light.
A lingual geologist whose
rocks of words open down inside a hole
that turns out to be

the sky itself.

3/5

DEATH CURVES INWARD

Death curves inward.
Everything curves inward as we
  go. The way a
flower curls and dies.

Failed marriages, businesses that
   don't turn out, ideals in youth eluding us,
the world unchanged, we left in our

underwear bewildered. Less

perfection and perfect ease in the outward,
up those stairs in a flash, less of that,
the sense of the world ours for the
   taking, gobbling its hors d'oeuvres on the
run, it's in more
measured doses, not that our

emperorship is not possible, but of a more
illumined island domain – glowing its
harbor, tangly its woods, hypnotic its
music – as we travel

inward to cockatoo call. There's a
light more somber where true
   encounters take place, the
     giddy smile exchanged for a

compassionate gaze of wonder in closer

league with things as they are,

where at the absolute center is mankind's
actually ever-present marriage of mortality and immortality

whose slowly waltzing skeletons we can
observe with silent joy. This

world only a preview, God's standing

invitation to come live and die

over all.

3/5

FLOWER SHOW

After a disappointing visit to the
   Philadelphia Flower Show
(wilted flowers in cardboard gardens)
I hit upon a Flower Show I'd
love to see: the actual and very real
mystic blue flower of Novalis, the *lichtblaue Blume*
in black vase in black
    room with
       single golden spotlight to
bring out its velvety depths, its
intoxicating splendor, flower of
       deepest longing.

A smallish, intimate room of rose displays, the
Sick Rose of Blake, destroyed in its
   "bed of crimson joy," straggly
battered petals
    hanging over a rock ledge –
Gertrude Stein's rose, so
    completely itself, so
itself itself itself
that it actually dangles suspended in
    air in
supreme solipsistic glory.

And most grandly and gruesomely, the
rose of Rilke that some say caused his death, blood
    still on its thorn, *"pure contradiction,*
joy to be nobody's sleep under

so many eyelids."

Then in another hall, Hart Crane's Air Plant, the
actual *"tuft that thrives on*
saline nothingness, inverted
　octopus with heavenward
arms, ventriloquist of the Blue!" with
　deep-sea underwater lights
　　swirling continuously
around it, arid and
　　ecstatic.

A special hall of daffodils, first
Wordsworth's naturally, a whole
field of the very ones he saw that day,
wandering lonely as a cloud,
"tossing their heads in sprightly dance" –
and lying in a book of pressed flowers, but
still sweet-scented, William Carlos Williams'
"asphodel, that greeny flower
　like a buttercup
　　upon its branching stem" he gave his
dear Floss.

Then, in another hall, *sunflowers!*
a few huge mad golden ones in a jug, Van Gogh's, the
true originals, spiky and
　Christ-crown-like, and to their left,
on a pile of twisted and rusted
　car-parts, railroad ties,
Ginsberg's very own sceptered sunflower,

*"crackly bleak and dusty
with the smut and smog and smoke of
olden locomotives in its eye"* – and
Blake's as well, bathed in a
sweet golden clime,
  "counting the steps of the Sun."

Then a tumultuous display of the
actual flowers of Rimbaud, *"some
resembling snouts
from which drool golden ointments
on the dark hair of buffalos,
calyxes full of fiery eggs,
downy thistles whose knots ten
  donkeys with burning eyes
labor to undo,
flowers that are chairs! Flowers almost
stones with gem-like tonsils,
and on a magnificent vermilion plate
stews of syrupy lilies,"* in a
hall the color of absinthe full of
soft groans and hundreds of loud flies.

Next to it, Baudelaire's *Fleurs du Mal*,
room filled with dark streets, cats and
mulatto women in see-through blouses with
  huge jangly earrings, accompanied by the
    faraway sounds of
doleful clarinets.

Then, facing these last two halls,

Whitman's lilacs, profusion of
   lilacs dripping and
blowing in the air, lucid and lubricious,
"tall-growing with heart-shaped leaves
    of rich green,
with many a pointed blossom rising delicate,
    with strong perfume –
every leaf a miracle –"
workmen with their
wives, and workmen with their
arms flung round each other,
   gazing –

Then, finally, in a magnificent glass hall all
    to itself, rising heavenward,
the great white rose of Dante's *Paradiso*, angels
     diving like
   bees upward into its
petals slowly rotating in the ceiling, streaming with

rays of silvery light, radiant white rose, vast and crystalline,
tier upon tier,

Beatrice at her petal station
smiling beatifically down –

"…fly with thine eyes this heavenly garden through!"

3/9

FIVE MINUTES TO LIVE

If I knew I had only five minutes to live
I wonder if I'd leave this page blank –
each poem that gets written seems like
    steam coming into the room from
        under death's door.
Faces appear in it, light and dark latticework
like blades of a fan working through it,
    propellers through an English fog.

Five minutes. The tunnel to God unblocked, great
rocks of time taken away from its mouth,
now possible to enter, venture in a few feet,
    get the feel of it, the last few

heartbeats and breaths, visions of the
outward eye and sounds to the outward ear,
before entering that other world entire.

Would, like leaving crumbs for birds or old
clothes in a box on the doorstep for someone to
take away, would I
have a sudden Lao-Tsu-ian quip that plunges to
the very bottom of the cataract of nature and
the soul? Or would a

pearl gray sky be the only legacy, with slow

cranes crossing it, way up high, and far away?

I often think it would be excellent to really decide to live as if
I had only one year left, do
all the things I torment and tease my soul to do,

somewhere between sitting down under a tree or
in a small whitewashed room
with only Qur'an and prayer mat, beads and a
notebook, and founding a theater of
Absurd Revelation, boisterous and
profound, puppets and musicians facing
out from our central green whirlwind to the gray world
    inviting people in.

But with only five minutes! I'd want to

lay my head down on desert sand,
draw with a spiral black line to the
center of the world

and dive in!

Or I might just
sit very still where I was
in the eternity of five minutes and let it all through.

Bug on the windowsill.
Phone ring.

Siren down the street.
Whippoorwill.

3/12

QUAIL IN THE GRASS

My father was a charming, uneducated
   man, who loved delicatessens.
Combed his jet black hair straight back,
jet black until it turned snow white.
Who had a pot belly while I was
   growing up, but after a
heart attack became thin and
stayed that way until he died.

He smiled often, had comical, gently
   teasing ways, until he was
too deaf to enter into conversation.
He often looked quizzical. Later
   uncomprehending. I think I generally
found him uncomprehending, and
didn't try too hard to make him comprehend.
I always found him locked in the
   20s, especially during the 60s.
Affable, he made affability into a
   fine art.

My father was a cork on water.
He was a slow horse with big hooves
   although he was a
smooth dancer, fox trot, waltz,
   loved Strauss, Jerome Kern,
was a poor man who worked hard to grow
rich. Worked day and night. Came home
late then went out to his

Freemasonic meetings in his red fez, inscrutable,

was generally secretive, though I never thought he
had that many secrets to hide. I

may have been wrong. I'll never know.

He was a door onto a
gravely arctic place. Standing

alone among elk. His song might go:

*"Hey, hey, I'm living on this earth,
can't imagine how I got here,
can't imagine where I'm going.*

*There's a quail in the grass there.
I hear a quail in the grass there."*

3/12

RED

Everyone has his or her own way of saying the word
   "red." Everyone
pronounces or mispronounces it according to
an inner truth.
Everyone sees red in his or her own way,
against a coral sky turning purple before
   going completely black,
on lips in glossy magazine photographs, with
  one tiny spotlit moisture sparkle,
in Jackson Pollock paintings, in looping strings as
   explosive energy winding across space,
on a rose or small carnation, any
way of the infinitely various ways red has of
turning up in the world, and

meets the outer perception with a deep inner
resonance all his or her own, elided with
imbedded associative rednesses, red
grandma lollipops, red top-down roadsters,
  sexy first kiss, first
  red shirt taken off one swoop over head,
   cold nipples at night turning
flesh red,

and so we are all self-contained universes, islands
interconnected but with
unique flora and fauna distinctively our own,
great elongating petals from rare
inner island orchids, great singing

cries from rare night creatures who
shuffle around in the dark aching for love.
Each of us pronounces or mispronounces, comprehends or
miscomprehends entire universes of
content, sidewise-slanted to all that is real, though
unfixed, just as

we are, invented by God each instant, inventing our
own engines for propelling redness, our
own white-aproned laboratories for
investigating the integrity of redness, the
resilience and unbeatability of
    just plain red, or the
effect of red in relation to mauve, teal,
    chartreuse, white, black and the
rippling combativeness between
brilliant strawberry red, say, and
a mustardy khaki color, or a pale, pale
    robin's egg blue,

although what I mean in all this is more the
beautiful isolated sad and somehow
totally redeemed human being we all are, living so
totally in our own universe that
has its own sunrises and lunar eclipses,
its own rainstorms and rainbows and
sees through the eyes of the beholder
just what beauties are to be seen going either
way in or way out,

and at the same time, in this grand huge bubble

in which we all live, walking around with
thought and speech balloons, saying
"red" in as many ways as there are of us,
there's a bright fountain in the middle, and
somehow we're both outside it and
in the middle of it at the same time,
fountain of superlative light, fountain of
   commonality, fountain of
     inverted domes flying
from the world of the unseen into our own,
fountain where *"red"* is from God, and
is filled, for all of us, with
God's divine energy, pouring through

thought and every word possible,
washing their billions of separate
blurred windows
   clean.

                                                            3/13

HOW TO EXTEND THE POEM FROM THE BODY

How to extend the poem from the body
   like a quicksilver that remains,
as permanent as a piece of furniture in a room,
   the placement of an object on a shelf,
     a wind.

An extension like speech, trailing from us, preceding
   us, remaining in the
     memory after we're gone, or a
shadow that exists in another world but is still
attached to us, and wouldn't
   exist at all without us,
or a way of walking, a gesture, quirk,

the poem a physical presence with
light coming out of its face, or dark
   hooded eyes, hair flowing or
unkempt,

speech unslurred, remarkable for the
high pitch of its clarity, words
   memorable as pearls on a string, each one
distinct from another, glittering,
a movement of our bodies in space
as if through panels of mist on which

ducks in flight over bronze ponds are painted,
seashore scenes where horizon enters heaven,
extensions of terrain past visibility, out into

    unknown territories that
turn out to be landscapes much like the
ones we see and easily comprehend, but only
    lack our continuing forward through time
      to actually be there.

That silver-blue skies over black lagoons where
    great white birds extend their wings
could flow around us and out of us as we
move on the earth in search of food, small
    comforts, breath-gusts of eternity,
that our stillness as well as our
movements be orchestrated with proper
choruses and crescendos.

That our sudden coming-home
surround us with the complimentary
ode through whose airy expostulations
actual leaves turn brown and
    fall to the ground
      tinged with sunset gold, to
pile in papery drifts at our feet, even before

a first word is uttered.

                                                3/14

AFTER A DREAM

After a dream like that I'm
   amazed I can walk! Lift my
body upright, stand, propel
     my two legs.
We're carried aloft in our mother's wombs
as well as a year or two after birth, and
not until we're transported on the royal palanquin
to our graves do we get such
   aerial service again.

In dream we fly. I used to ascend
between telephone wires waving my arms.

We float, run at terrific speeds,
become disembodied, bodiless consciousness
witnessing whatever's in front of us,

then get back into our bodies, if we can
walk at all, if we're not paraplegic, and
stand up and walk, all neurological
zaps and triggers in physical place
unthinkingly, maneuvering us
forward, or sidewise, crablike, or in some cases,
backward, with complete ease.

Put all our weight on those
comical tree roots, our feet,
funny little ten-toed animal paws,
hit the floor, support the inner skeleton and

fleshy wrap, the
robot brain captained by stereoscopic
eyes in their comfy cabins on top, to avoid
furniture and navigate through doors –

what a conglomeration of miracles!

What God-sends, these nonchalant
anatomical abilities!

3/16

ARCHIPELAGOS

"I'm exploring the archipelagos of my mind," he said
grandiloquently.

We hoped he wouldn't be long, perched, as we
    were, on a precarious
        ledge.

Was he working on chess moves, engaging in high
    mathematics, remembering
    complicated lists, recalling word for word
passages from arcane literature?
Did our lives depend on the outcome?

Yes, damn it, our lives *did* depend on the outcome,
forcing us to do the same,
me wondering how I wound up in such a fix,
the river waters crashing
    mindlessly below us. Or was it,

as I began to wonder to myself, *"mindlessly,"*
did that small but crucial boulder dislodge from
beneath my left foot "mindlessly," breathtakingly
descending through sheerest air to a
long way down, completely "mindless?"

We held onto each other very tightly, my
fellow travelers certainly were applying their
minds to this predicament.

But I began to notice a certain
mouse-brain inquisitiveness about just about
everything around me, inquisitiveness, I mean, where
things like the sage-like brush on this ledge, jutting
way out over the abyss, almost has a
look of wonder on its, well, not "face" exactly, but
in its whole being, from interior-most to
exterior-most – or the great vast

space between us and certain death, it also, now
to my sense of things, at least, had a kind of
intelligent *"let's-wait-and-see-what
   happens-next"* look to it, as if
      space had a "look," a
kind of aspect, but perhaps it was just
me not wanting to hurtle to my
death through just plain stupid space, but
   rather through an intellectually
      aware element…
hmmm, perhaps.

Our bodies were getting so tense in their
frozen positions I really didn't know how much
longer we'd all be able to last this way, when he
suddenly burst out: *"No mind to explore!"*

and moved forward, us, stiffly at first,
following.

And oh! It felt so fine!

I felt we were of the same mind.

And of the waters, and the wind.

3/17

YOU OPEN A DOOR AND IT'S A STARRY NIGHT

Wildflowers on either side of the road
   so yellow they're neon,

escalators out of the clouds, each step inhabited by
    mammals and birds from the tropics,
      intent on ascending,

a two-headed man who comes into the room,
   asks a question then answers it,

God's sacred miracles hidden unseen in the world, and
His visible, simple ones like air, rain, music,
   breathing, and the
     fact that they're one and the same,

a very black intricately carved lacquered fan
   recording mankind's history through the ages,
    easily collapsible, useful in
      hot weather,

every food by every ethnic people on earth laid out
in a kind of mile-long smörgasbord, up hill and
   down dale, and you can
     walk along sampling each one, a smiling
ethnic representative standing behind each one
      telling you its name,
a light-show of special light effects
at the beginning of creation, a
    similar one of the light-effects at the

  end,

a concert of cosmic sounds from the same moment, low rumbling
  crash and crescendo at first,
eternal crescendo at the end, fading in rivers of waves into
  infinity,

the voice of my beloved whispering something
  into my ear, barely understood, a healing nevertheless,

a sky full of small circular rainbows like
  pinwheels, small enough to see the
radiant sheen of their entire circumference spinning,

a door you open and it's a starry night,

a door you open and you're deep in the Amazon,

a door you open and you're in the
  company of the saints, known and
    unknown, recognizable as well as
anonymous,

birds with human faces, singing melodies of unearthly beauty
as they swoop through trees, rare gems in a purple twilight,

small alleyways that curve behind buildings
  where shops you've never seen before
    sell objects you've only
      imagined,

cities of slowly revolving silvery contraptions that
cure the soul's ills upon witnessing them,

a scarf you can throw over anything and it'll
    turn to pure light,

this poem come back in visual terms only,

this poem represented by singing voices only,

this poem expressed by various
timbres and intonations of

total silence only.

                                                          3/18

SMALL PARABLE

A little river ran down the
    side of a mountain, content,
to just be what it was. It was even just
    called: *a river.*

Put a person on earth and they want
    horns to toot and
whistles to blow for them, and for

everyone to lose interest in
    everything else.

                                                    3/19

TO PROCLAIM HIS NEWS

for Hamza Yusuf Hanson

To proclaim his news, some of it
   grabbed out of the air with a pair of
kaleidoscopes with telescopic lenses,
some teased from a small glass box full of
green fire, he

felt he had to go to the highest plateau possible
to have the necessary vantage to
be heard. He

put on his hat and coat, slipped the
fish into his pocket, and
set out. As he

walked and walked through the glare of the
afternoon sunlight, feeling the
   importance of his news dwindle in the
blare of billboards and yelling boys, and

walked and walked through the golden
twilight feeling some of the glamour return
even as the vast night made him feel more like a
twitching bug crawling across a greasy floor,

(who would hear his melodic cries, how would
  the winds carry them to their
    intended destination: the ears of the hearts of the

populace he so loved but whose
faces were hidden behind newspapers or
blurred by speeding through dwindling time?)

He walked all night, and as the
dawn flicked the sky-switch a lighter
shade of black, then purple, then indigo
    slipping finally into baby blue,
he found himself alone on a high plateau

and the early chill stung his cheeks
and cracked his lips, and a

rabbit long-leggedly hopped into a grass-clump
and the first birds of morning sang
and the gradual light illuminated the
trail and the pebbles, trees and knolls

and off in the distant haze
those he would soliloquize.

                                                  3/21

OF MY MOTHER, 92, WITH ALZHEIMERS

1

I hate to think she may no longer dream of me.

She lies on her couch and stares at the ceiling
  like a bird. Blinks and keeps
staring. Her arthritic fingers like bird claws.
But her face also reminds me of a cat's,
looking completely with seemingly unseeing
    eyes. Then comprehending. Then
not comprehending. Her

frail, cold form, cheeks sunken, hair so usually
carefully kempt, now spreading out white and
lank and long behind her head on the
pillow, hair I'd never seen not in some
beauty shop cut, now left to
    nature, oblivious to fashion. Ancient.
Crone hair. Mother, my dear affectionate
mother, a crone. But a

sweet crone. *"Should I be here? Is this
where I'm supposed to be?"*

Blinks. Recognizes. Loses the
    thread.
There on her perch in a kind of
    silvery nowhere. Who

took me downtown to the movies, by bus, later by
car, who dressed me warmly, snapping the
   leather strap of my
     cap under my chin, who
took me across the Bay Bridge to
San Francisco on the train (the span under the
automobile level above), and I

remember so pungently the smell of the
Hills Brother Coffee factory on the
San Francisco side, and the
   coffee cup up-tilted ecstatic
Arab in yellow robe and white turban bigger than
life on the billboard. That was my

mother who took me there, who tilted her
head and smiled, and flirted, and hated her
round gray mother for flirting, and she even

now flirts on the bed, face up at me, winking,

frowning, opening eyes wide, pulling down her
mouth, then smiling that heartbreaking

mother's smile. My

mother's smile.

2

The Prophet Muhammad said Paradise lies at the
    feet of mothers, and I
know it's true.
My mother lies there with
Paradise at her feet, frail feet now in
soft moccasins, barely able to get her to the
bathroom with her aluminum walker for support,
her thin blue-scribbled legs, whiter than paper,
yet Paradise is there. She

spoon-fed me. That's the
fountains of Paradise. She
held me close, that's the
affection of Paradise, and worried herself to
death about me, and had the
dread despair, and was so

glad when I called, and looked into my
face now long and hard and
put her arms around my
neck with extraordinary almost vicelike
grip to kiss me, and though her

kiss, so dry, so cold, lips weathered, was
the kiss of death, on me and on her, it was the
kiss of life, a mother's kiss, which is the

endlessly flowing rivers of Paradise with a
supernatural light flickering along their ripples,

and the air of Paradise is the mother's atmosphere,
where she walks, where she

lies stretched out now, hands plucking a
coverlet, veiled eyes fastened on the
ceiling, already more in

Paradise than here. O God, may You

take her there!

3

Silver-haired Siberian mothers!

Hoolah!

Stalking snow-deer, a bone clenched between their teeth,
silver eyes clenched against
    storm, determined to get there!

Hoobah!

Natural Wisconsin mothers on cow farms in denim
    skirts and boots of rough leather, rope
burns on hands, faces of raw cow milk,
cheeks of burnt straw, eyes of hot
    water!

Ooyah!

Moccasin mothers against high winds putting
feather skin capes over moon-faced papooses,
cowering in teepee dark, hearts beating deep,

Cachaw!

Mothers in circle making quilt, toothless,
   once-beautiful, lissome,
nimble-fingered, breasts bone, breasts now
    dry as bone,
lonesome in their plenitude,

Bashah!

Mothers and more mothers, floating horizontal, head to
toe, great rings of them revolving
   around the globe!

Hooshah!

Mothers everywhere!

Living in wood crates on Chinese docks,
palaces with carpets five inches thick,
  high rises, tenements,
the projects, the dumps, scrounging supermarket
   tips, dipping croissants in
thick cream in outdoor Parisian cafés to feed their
young, birds in the air, mouse mothers in
holes, my mother in

California waiting patiently for
death.

*"Should I be here? Where
should I be? Is this all right? What
are you going to do now?"*

"I'm just going to sit with you for a while,
   mom. I'm just going to
hang out with you for awhile."

"OK."

4/1

MOCKINGBIRD OUTSIDE MY WINDOW

for Susan Growe

Oh blue dozens and sassafras designs, a
mockingbird outside my window makes me happy!

Its yearly visit. Enigmatic singer, brother,
drunkard just like me, under our skins!

En route, you take to a high tree or telephone pole,
ruler of all you survey, just for a moment, and

sing till your feathers tremble. *Look, I'm
addressing you!* Sitting on bedside. Having

just arrived from out-of-town dreams.
Perched here, but no ruler. Surveying our

congeneity. I could
take off, leaving you to

shower, shave, dab deodorant, drive to work
and worry. I could

chirp and warble, let you do the telephone-talking, the
up and down stairs walking (you'd probably hop),

wring your wingtips until the job got done.

But, nah, you're the bird, I'm the man,

a bird's gotta do what a bird's gotta do,

to sing a while. Stay for a day or two.
I'll force my two bird feet in shoes and

shuffle on.

You excel in song.

4/2

JERUSALEM

Seven yellow things stood up to champion the
   color yellow.
They were in different parts of the room, so the
total effect was of a significant majority.
But three beetles (actually they were
   cockroaches), thought this might be a
good time to put in a good word for cockroaches.
They were booed resoundingly and so
scampered back behind the bleach bottle.

Quadrilateral space took it upon itself to
display its largesse, its come-what-may attitude, its
absolute liberality, that anything capable of being a thing
was welcome to be that thing in its domain.
So a sound out of nowhere, a pure
note as if plucked from the well of silence and
flung into quadrilateral space
opened itself into screens and levels and
   unfoldings so marvelous and complex that
actual historical events began flickering visually
in the concave bowl of its presence,

caravan routes through Mecca when there was
only the Ka'bah and the well of Zamzam,

flute sound and the jangle of camel bells,
hobnail-boots-on-cobblestones rhapsody when
Poland was invaded by the S.S. of Germany,
the sound of bee's wings as it discovers nectar,

  sliding way down in and snuffling around,
the high-pitched symphonic sound of all
orchestral instruments playing octaves of a
  single note together,
a chair shuffled to the center of the room, its
  four legs actually scraping the hardwood.

"Gentlemen… and lady," it began,
  throwing itself back a little with an
   air of authority, winking at the
feminine window that was letting the breezes of the
sunny day into the room through her
  wide openness,

"we have a universe, and we are a universe.
If you hear the clopping of hooves, think of a
  zebra.
If I fall out of the sky does that make me a
  heavenly body?"

The room became still. All this
declarative assertion of self was
too much for it. The sound that had
made such a dramatic entrance
wavered, since it was made up of waves, then it
became as slender as a hair, and

a gorgeous goddess-of-rare-beauty type
slowly turned out of it to face us, opened
eyes so vast the sound and sight of ocean-crash
  could be made out in their pupils.

Suddenly this room with so much political weight and
    such high political stakes
became a meadow, and she a

shepherdess moving slowly with her
fluffy flock to a nearby stream glistening in the
noon light, and yellow
was itself perfect shades of yellow dotted in the wildflowers, all the
bugs ran freely through the
    grass blades and stalks,
space was wider than could be
    encompassed by our perception of it
and all the sounds of the universe, small as it
    is, resoundingly praised the
Creator of all this, a hum audible

on the shepherdess' pale lips as she
bent down to the clear stream, then caught
sight of her face, paused for a moment, and

drank.

                                                      4/4

RECORDING ANGELS

A zillion pencils, made of celestial stuff.
A trained staff? No, somehow
two do the trick, one on the right shoulder hopefully
    writer's cramped from
too much scribbling of good acts,

the one on the left shoulder with writer's block I hope
or so blessedly indulgent… but actually
they have no editorial minds of their own, and
are reflections of cosmic law, the
    crystalline pattern of things-as-they-are
in which if a lie is spoken a lie is recorded, since
a lie is a house of cards or a domino effect
that ripples through reality and affects so
many labyrinthine details, the angel on the left simply
has to record it in its rawest form, plain as a
wart, *as is!*

I hope my recording angels are happy.

The one on the left
has too much to do, and is made
unhappy from having to do it. Unhappy
for my sake. And I hope the

one on the right catches all those subtle little
details, stray good thoughts, tick-tock
moments of remembrance of God, those good-natured
smiles for others said to be charity as much as

giving money away, *I'm
banking on it!* Blending blue

winds that surround them, blinding white
light all around them, blessed angelic

    state they're in!

4/5

DUE PROPORTION

If it's a locomotive faster than a speeding bullet
it's faster still,

if it's a bloom with myriad blossoms
the air it blooms in's more beautiful,

if it's a deep heart's response to love
it's miles deeper still,

if it's a word that sets the world on fire
its brightness and heat does
    both worlds fill.

We move through space to our destinies
that seem out of reach and invisible.

Who knows what we'll say next or
    how we'll be, soft or
        shrill,

if we'll stand or sit, laugh or weep,
    live long or lie still.

The room we walk into's already there,
so's cemetery hill.

The window we look out of's surrounded by a
vast window sill.

The sky we see's only microscopic
against the heaven of the Angel Gabriel.

4/8

TRACES

Traces that linger in the air long after
what made them are no longer there,
traces around the

crumpled sidewalk body, chalk-outlined, a
blood red splotch, broken glasses by the
hydrant, traces of a memory-jogging fragrance up a

glittering stairway onto the mezzanine, something
elusive hanging in the air, visual traces as when

either my eyesight is failing me or that
chair just turned into a quick black cat and
ran from the room, traces of our

voices, the way they echo even after we're done,
traces in our ear canals, traces of our
voices themselves like record grooves
traced in the walls we lived between, played eons

later by intrepid archeologists, they'd get
whole conversations, ghostly banalities,
Edison wax cylinder mysteriousness of the
effective and affecting sounds of our voices, people
now skeletons, gap-faced, deep in the soil,

like a desert camp pulled up its stakes and gone,
a campfire smoldering, a peg or two left split in the
sand, we leave our traces, we

follow traces left by those before us as we seek out
traces of a Greater Being, like reading jet-streams in
clouds, like news on the lips of those who can't

quite shake the memory of the impact, having
left its traces in the way the faces glow of
those left behind in the holy aftermath,
something forever changed

from mere traces!

4/10

BEHEMOTH IN THE MOUTH

"There's a darkness in your mouth, and
    beneath it a Behemoth."
Where can I go from such a phrase, where
will it lead? Something about

resonant indicators, blue steam around
crystals of meaning, out of pitch
darkness, coming forward into true

presence from the wet human caverns of the
heart, larynx, the very

air we inhabit, place of angels hovering
just above beasts, their
  concerned Blakean faces gazing long and
hard into the shaggy roughness such
hearts represent. A

deep-down darkness, not of ash, but of
the creative murk from which such things as
stars emerge, blown out into radiance.

Without that darkness no star would be, could be
born into spatial exuberance of being,

in the same way in that deep down darkness in your
mouth whole splendid illuminations
unscroll themselves, to ignite us, and

underneath that darkness dwells one of God's
creatures of the deeps, who rears up, face of
tar, face of lava, wipes out whole
villages, riles up whole oceans if it's riled,

then flutter of wings that cut across it, furtive
streaks across the dark,

wing-tips visible or felt, their
inexplicable touch!

4/12

LEAVES

I went for a walk in the woods
and all the new Spring leaves were notes of music.

Each one in the air as a result of its own
  unfurling, blending with those
urban echoes, distant dog barks,
  car-door slams, call and repeat of
quail, flutter in the trees, air
  scintillant with light, and then

heard blossom clusters out of deep vermillion pods
like clusters of notes, miniature oratorios of
chords, polyphonous with other
blossoms on the branch. It was so

bright there, Easter Sunday morning, happy for
people in their pews, the new leaves really

singing! As I write it now it becomes more
mental. But in their space those leaves

were singing!

                                                      4/12

GRAVITY

Everywhere on earth gravity is basically the
    same.
Drop a pin, a shirt button, a dime, a
feather, they float or fall to the ground,
    lost in the rug-twill.
Drop a piano, an obelisk, a tractor-trailer, a four-story
house, and they fall, crack upon
    impact, splinter, roar and
crumble to pieces. Gravity. Basically

everywhere the same.

Drop a coconut in thick Borneo rain forest, an
ancient Babylonian gold leaf crown just
    rescued from a tomb, Walt Whitman's
brain, they smash to pieces because they
can't just fall through the center of the
earth and out again into space on the
other side sailing forever.

Drop someone with a well-aimed bullet to the
heart, or major cardiac infarction, or
scimitar to the bared neck, or just
dizziness from too much wine and heavy dancing

and the full figure falls to the floor, felled like a
tree, face down or face up, horizontal,
hugging gravity like a lover.

Same in Mongolia,
downtown Los Angeles, Tierra del Fuego,
leaf, log, lava, laughing man, laughing woman,
all groundward go.

So, if this is so, this simple fact of physics, it might
unite us in the knowledge we all
follow the laws of physics till we're
all laid low. All of us on earth

trying to stand tall.
Leaf or Lithuanian.

Before the Fall.

4/13

ON TOUR

for Ann Rasmussen

Trumpets were laying in a pile at the
    bottom of the hill.
Drum skins floated like lily pads on the
    pond.
Violins were stuck neck down in the ground.
The cello'd become a rabbit hutch already
    bursting.
Trombones rested on each other like a subway diagram,
clarinets like black walking sticks waiting for their
    users to arrive,
the empty bus with its doors wide open and its
    motor running,

for now the musicians were playing the
leaves of trees, stones, all
    flat or round surfaces,
branches fallen to the base of trees, bits of
bark struck against rock,

and they sang the air, they
tuned the air into song,

God's air became praise of He Whose it is,

every gnat notes, every
thin line of light a staff.

Music echo'd from that hill with no
musician in sight.

They'd all disappeared into the music.

Now the music of space was who they were.

4/20

THE POET'S VISION

We've swung away from the poet's vision –
We want to get to the moon, mars.

The poets got us there before
without the use of oars.

HOW IT COMES

1

I haven't the vaguest idea how it happens.
I'm sitting somewhere, my belly bulging,
hands with liver spots in some
    nonchalant gesture, usual
consciousness with its various line by line
    translations, shifts of attention, blank
spots, and
all of a sudden as if the
    earth jerked on its axis, a
strong thought imposes itself, or a single line, with a big
echo behind it, space in a shape like a shadow behind it,
which are the rest of the lines of the poem awaiting their
entrance cues, which actually don't
take place until some words like these
lumber or actually
figure-skate in with the sound of
pen point on paper being the sound
    skate-blades make on ice, that
small hard scraping sound.

A blond hill exposes its sunlit banks to
us or a wisp in the air that sort of
turns in the light to show off a
floating continent fully populated with the
best of creatures, men and
women singing glossolalic songs, mythic beasts,
    palm trees whispering,

but it all comes out of God's night as if a great
invisible hand had let
   go of a butterfly that

flitters over an abyss. Deep purple
rifts going straight down. Loud water below.

And a meaning attached, bubbling along,
lifting everything's spirits off the
ground a little, and while the
fit is on I'm not quite human, don't
   interrupt me, I'm
far smarter than usual, and the
   world is zigzagging back and
forth like a heart-dial, clanging metal pinball
   bouncing off flippers,
thoughts like illuminated islands
set down on black water, shedding
circles of soft lemon light, circle after
   circle, to the far edge of darkness.

Roses bloom spontaneously. Gorgeous golden
Africans appear. Spiritual
   insight spreads its vistas on
this side of the mirror-world, no blue
   smoke interposes its
face-shapes of the
infamous and famous in the air.

You feel you could go anywhere.

2

Where does it come from, and
where does it go? It comes from
God's nowhere, and goes
    back again. En route it
passes through us like those long linen strips through a
Yogi's nostrils drawn
    deep into his bowels.

You can't hold onto it, drunk or starved, it's
whole point is translucence, transience and transcendence,
a wind, ah, a wonderful
wind, like a *djinn* dancing happily in the
middle of the room, showering us pictures that
maybe if we follow we'll come out on the
Paradise side, maybe on the Hell. But the

pure heart is paramount. It sits on its cubical throne
like a muffled tom-tom, its
thoughts hieroglyphics set to music, great
swans moving on greater lakes,
great necks bending to an unseen logic
greater than us all.

The universe bodies forth
then withdraws. We sip the entire

ocean both of stars and deeper currents
through these tiny straws.

                                        4/24

HOW THE UNIVERSE WORKS

To find out how the universe works
bring a little silver wrench, a pen that
    bursts into flame, a horse with doe eyes and
shimmering whiteness and sit here next to me on a
windowsill on a night of sonorous thunder,
    between one breath and the next, watch
dust motes intently as they mix and fall, rise and
      twist in any light, invisible in the
          dark. Have faith above all, as the

huge puzzle pieces of the mountains fit
snugly into the interlocking pieces of the sky, that
water fill your cup, that your
cup flow over before it goes dry, that a
perfect moon throw its
    light over your repose as well as your

waking, that black roses give way to red,
that one black rose approach you and as you
gaze into its opening folds of petals
the face of the true love you've looked for forever
open its eyes to gaze back at you,

and it will be not the elusive dream of your
fragmented imaginings, but the
ones always around you now, their too-familiar
    faces, the original desert stretched
      all the way back to the
beginning, when dawn broke its egg and bled

scarlet on blank sand.

Between one breath and the next
a billion sudden flights, a billion safe
    landings, between

one breath and the next
the universe unfolded like an origami bird
    deconstructed before you.

Night follows day. The opposites collide and
mate. Day follows night and their
hectic progeny appear.

Your face as it sinks on the pillow, exhausted and
relieved. The burdens like

petals, fallen in drifts then
blown away.

4/26

REMEMBER YOUR ORIGIN AND GOAL

Remember your origin and goal
whenever daylight hits your floor,
when a door opens to let in air,
when the air is full and night is long,
when a butterfly flies like an
   ignited origami in the air, whenever a

leaf falls or rhododendron
bursts into purple flame, when
nothing happens at all, remember Him then,
His Might and Majesty, Beauty, and
  all His Names,

when a baby cries, a boat sails, a bird
sails in the sky, a road leads
down to the sea, ocean waves pile on
top of each other like shingles on a roof,
   slopes of
      relentless
energy, flash in a pale sun,

sea-birds' cry, remember Him then, the
long flat sea, the far horizon,
     endless sky,

remember our Origin then, and how we've
come this far, or not so far,
come to a stop or still moving, remember in

movement or stillness, the piston's pull and
thrust, machinery's groan or purr, around that
bend or on that straightaway,

curled in a furry ball at the base of a tree,
flying above the highest tree, leaf floor, carpet of
golden leaves, dead leaves, remember in
life and death, just before death takes all,
pulls in the drawer, when
no more remembrance takes place, all our
luminous letters sent, ignited envelopes
    arcing through heaven,

our heart an echoing mud mosque in a
hot country, solitary
believer sitting against a wall doing the
ninety-nine beads,

face of night full of sweet compassion,
lips in constant remembrance,

until *we're* remembered,
until we sit still on any available edge

and remember.

                                             4/29-30

WHY I WANT LI-YOUNG LEE TO SEND ME THE POEM HE READ TO ME OVER THE TELEPHONE

for Li-Young Lee

He'd just written it. It shimmered with a
numinous newness. Ecstatic electric
nimbus that surrounds all real births. It
cried. Its cry could be heard

all the way down the hall to the
waiting room. And the poem made my
heart a waiting room that didn't even know
a moment before what it was
waiting for. That's how

real it was, how honest an
explosion out of his neurological pathways
which like flutes were open conduits for sweet
light to blow through.

To my unexpected ear.

In it his father eternally rowed in a boat through his
death to a deeply felt fate, his
wife said *"ha ha"* and his
God elusively shadow-stalked belief's
deep conundrum for him in the last line. But

I can't be completely sure of these images. The
lines aren't in front of me, a cinematic flicker on

blank screen is all I've retained, and of course
his voice, since he'd just written it, the
pent-up sluice had just broken through, his
voice exultant, incredulous, like
a man saying *"I love you"* after sex, throaty,
post-ecstatic, still
vibrating, heart to

heart through those miraculous telephone
wires from Chicago to Philadelphia. Who knows what

scatterings of birds fluttering onto the lines,
what cloud-shapes hovering above the
electronic transmission that truly
etched a brown tintype of shadowy movement
in a new area of my brain, and

I long to revisit it, even though it be
paler on the page,

rekindle some of its pure primordial notes, its
two flutes tuned slightly apart and blown
simultaneously, the poem I heard then and

the one I could hold in my hand and
read with my eyes, slightly discordant soulful

notes blending into a single music.

4/30

LUNAR DAY

We all go to our separate beds like mummies,
stretch ourselves out, faces to the ceiling,

lovers, soldiers, epileptics, kings,
each alone on a soft slab, each in an

enclosed room, stretched out asleep for
eternity in the

tilted cosmos of our dreams, enveloping
globe of consciousness that shimmers as it

surrounds the world. Bubble of
human babble that actually

connects us, one gorgeous mind with a
zillion facets, turning so slowly in

solar night, trailing a banner of light
behind it into lunar day.

ALL MY LIFE

for Hakim Archuletta

I've lived in the same house all my life.
I know it looks out on a bare soccer field.

From one window you can see mountain.
The door opens on dry scrub. A

mountain lion's face sometimes fills one window.
My mother gave birth to me here. I

romped through the rooms. I was
sent to my room. I was

alone there. And not alone.
I heard God's silence in that room. His

companionable voice. It
spilled out like white flowers.

I grew taller later, deeper voiced, sexual.
A circus came and lived there. I fell in

love with a horse, a clown's face, a
tightrope walker in silver dress, a

spotlight, the secret caverns in the dark at the
ceiling of the tent, the off-key *oompah* orchestra,

the sound of wind beating against canvas,
the face of a tiger filling the bars of his cage.

Now I am old, and the circus is gone.
My wife weaves a tapestry to cover us both,

seated on a chair.
Sometimes the face of an angel appears in her

face. It lights up the rooms.
Her companionable voice lights up the rooms.

Dark corners under the eaves and the
emptiness of the rooms are still.

The roof is open to the sky.
I wonder if I shall leave through the door, through

a window where the wild lion-face appears
from time to time or through the roof open to the sky.

Some float straight out into the night
and are gone.

You'll recognize the house when you come.
Singing birds draw you in.

5/5

OCEAN POETRY

I opened a blue hardcover book downstairs at my
favorite used bookstore that was an
anthology of sea poetry, read a few
poems, flipped pages, then

put it back on the shelf disappointed. Mostly
rhymed verses about the sea, or ships through waters in
    heroic progress, or
traditional sea-shanties, but I couldn't hear

the sizzle and resizzle of surf, bird cry flashing against
gray-white sky, the lines of the
poems didn't extend past their
regular margins at either side to show at least
inlets of intense blue leading to the great flat
ocean beyond, salt-stink of fish rot or
    polyp, salt air,

rock echo of great whoosh-sound of waters
crashing and recrashing against them, long
surf aftermath before repeated wave-crash,
the way light flattens into
    horizontals above ocean glare,
piles of light like mountains pale as glass at the
far horizon, how the sea-tides may change, wax and
wane, but the rhythm's always there, at the

end of town or down by the beach, as it was in
San Francisco when I lived there, walk through

Golden Gate park to the end and there's the
Pacific like a brown slate burnished miraculous gold under
bronze sunlight, or

in Gloucester going to find Charles Olsen, he
gone for the weekend, but looked out on his
ocean which somehow he'd invented, almost

big as he was, met him later in a tiny
coffee house in San Francisco,
  over six feet of walrus man with
eyebrows like coal barges and little
Ben Franklin pony tail, oceans inside him,
Atlantic history and myth-making inside him,
Maximus vision both outside and
    inside him,

and I could say there are oceans inside us, but it may seem
more like indoor swimming pools smelling of
   chlorine with echoes of swimmers shouting,

or I might say my
turquoise ring contains the entire ocean, black flickers
   down inside it hiding
     gentle monsters of the deep, or that the

sky also is an ocean,
no visible seams but an ever-extending
    fabric, going

way past the edges of its margins, and that

deep currents run through all of us as if we were also
a seafaring tribe in a bright magenta sunset
rowing a catamaran to holy music over the
sea of our souls under the sea of the sky.

The sea rolling black in the darkness, growling and
never still, the sea like the dew-bejeweled
eyelashes of a lover opening at dawn to thin
slivers of light, illuminating crests and rapid creatures

as the unstopping sea goes on rolling, under
   bright daylight, just as it

rolls unceasingly under cover of night.

5/7

CONSCIOUS THOUGHT PROCESSES

All the little treasures, things cherished,
looked at, turned around slowly in a

strong light, brought close to the eye, held
at arm's length and admired, set

down on white cloth and gazed at for
hours, bits of Roman cornice, mummified

goat cheese, glass eyeball from a
pirate ship, ormolu inlay, phosphorus about to ignite,

things fused by electrical catastrophe,
things liberated from their enclosing rock and

bathed in the air,
things tossed aside by emperors, pencil stub used to

write a masterpiece in prison,
first tin foil to reflect back an image of the

sun,

small ceramic arm as white as soap from the
first century,

each like a thought the sea might think,
thrown up from some arcane depth, propelled by a wave,

floated on foam, little treasured
objects like tics in a thought process,
blurted out into material existence, hand-
fashioned, lathe-turned, gem-tumbled,

meticulously carved, hewn, hammered together,
held up in the light

the same way mountains rising into majestic sky,
sheer cliffs plummeting to roaring

cataracts below, ocean sliding waters across
waters over all the earth, filling its

basins, jewels of glaciers, rainbow-crested waterfalls,
the unknown dimensions of space itself

displaying the conscious
thought processes of their Creator.

LOVE'S NOT MEANT TO BE EASY

"Love's not meant to be easy,
death's not meant to be hard,
life's a puddle of gold fish"
saith the bewildered bard.

"Make full use of sunbeams,
dip your donut in dew,
wipe that smile off your face
if you plan to be permanently blue.

Dream with the fury of fire,
live like a waterfall,
go down the rocks like a bubble
that's not being bothered at all."

"Easy to say," said the snowman,
weeping at the first sign of Spring,
"easy to say," said the day lily,
seeing night enter the ring.

The night's not so bad once you know
how to see with your feet and your hands,
time's not so bad once you stop
counting each grain of sand.

Everything's got forward motion,
the next world is getting nearer,
It's been said a thousand times
but there may be only one hearer.

"Ah well," said the bard, *"sing your song,
say your piece, wear your hair, get going,
raise your umbrella in rain-time,
take out your shovel when it's snowing."*

He rode off beyond the horizon,
he threw his hat in the air,
it glowed very white and moonlike,
for all I know it's still there.

A POETICS

I envision a rigorous poetry like the flashing
white columns of a classical building,
shooting up at each side of blackness, thick and
    tapered, flowering into arching
        fronds at top, shimmering marble-like with
silver flecks reflecting white sunlight,

and from the deep blackness between them
to the thrum of drum and bass strings,
figures of such overwhelming beauty, bronze
   skin, topaz eyes, lips in constant
remembrance, hearts like communicating
tambourines, feet in wooden sandals, proceeding

forward from the depths of the blackness,
hands raised at their sides, each one
representing a state of mind, an affection of the heart,
each one singing out its own song.

I think the Mexicans had it, but I'd not
    sacrifice the winner,
the North American tribes in the farthest north had it,
    but I'd probably not last out the winter,
the freshest interpretations of how the diviner's
    bones fly in the air and
fall in configurations of splendor
that the eye of the heart sees ruby red,

burning eye at the center of the heart

that cuts through dross

and looks out across plains and tumultuous tundra
and calls it good

and the dead fly into its mouth
as into the mouth of

Brahma in the Bhagavad Gita

and still call it good.

5/12

ROSES OF TIME

Brutal roses of time!
You bloom with your rare beauty
and are gone! From tight-fisted
bulbs unfurling petal by petal into
rose-red velvet, otherworldly
   fragrance, our

momentary joys making us so hopeful
that the world will turn its best face to us
and all our patient tenaciousness will
bear fruit, that the

moment will open like a room we can
live in, putting in our personal furniture,
a table, a vase of roses, you
   roses of time, stuck in a
vase!

Tomorrow you're dead, your red, red petals
like brown islands around the vase's base on
   the bare table in the
room that closes back inside our flesh
that also, like those petals, curls and
    fades.

Rose redness, rose sweetness, roseness itself on
thorny stems, out of nowhere
   blooming!

God's darlings.

Time's kisses blown to us
from a passing float!

>   5/18

SHEEP OF THE NIGHT

The light wind that bore Penelope's name
  over icy waves carved to points
bears Yours, haunted by echoes, owls
   blinking between beats, hills of

white horses, animated flecks against green under
a blinding blue sky, white statues on white
pedestals, carved lips not

repeating Your Name as my live heartbeats do, as the
fall of cones to the ground does, thud, then
   quiet, then another

word making its natural syntax and context in the
logorrhea of this place, unquiet with
comings and goings, forgetting Your

Presence then recalling, and with
recall comes every memory ever had on its
collective trade wind, trinkets from

Atlantis itself washed up on these
accessible shores of consciousness. I see a
green bird like a flash of emerald go by,
I see the signing of the Magna Carta and my

son's future graduation Magna Cum Laude, not all
boats have left safe harbor, the air is

thick with thought and butterflies, each
twinkling like foil in a bitter sunlight, bitter for
   falling on the just and the
     unjust alike, judgment remaining
God's alone, our feebleness too

wretched to decide, a fan of smoke thrown
up against a backdrop of fire,

Your Name repeated by each
crackle of flame, my
heartbeats in my mouth calling Your Name
on a hillside covered with sheep,

sheep of the night folding down,

sleep of the night furling in

in peaceable curls.

                                             5/23

ABOUT THE AUTHOR

Born in 1940 in Oakland, California, Daniel Abdal-Hayy Moore's first book of poems, *Dawn Visions*, was published by Lawrence Ferlinghetti of City Lights Books, San Francisco, in 1964, and the second in 1972, *Burnt Heart/Ode to the War Dead*. He created and directed *The Floating Lotus Magic Opera Company* in Berkeley, California in the late 60s, and presented two major productions, *The Walls Are Running Blood*, and *Bliss Apocalypse*. He became a Sufi Muslim in 1970, performed the Hajj in 1972, and lived and traveled throughout Morocco, Spain, Algeria and Nigeria, landing in California and publishing *The Desert is the Only Way Out*, and *Chronicles of Akhira* in the early 80s (Zilzal Press). Residing in Philadelphia since 1990, in 1996 he published *The Ramadan Sonnets* (Jusoor/City Lights), and in 2002, *The Blind Beekeeper* (Jusoor/Syracuse University Press). He has been the major editor for a number of works, including *The Burdah* of Shaykh Busiri, translated by Shaykh Hamza Yusuf, and the poetry of Palestinian poet, Mahmoud Darwish, translated by Munir Akash. He is also widely published on the worldwide web: *The American Muslim, DeenPort*, and his own website: www.danielmoorepoetry.com, and poetry blog: www.ecstaticxchange.wordpress.com, among others. He is also currently poetry editor for *Seasons Journal* and *Islamica Magazine*. The *Ecstatic Exchange Series* is bringing out the extensive body of his works of poetry (a complete list of published works on page 2).

POETIC WORKS by Daniel Abdal-Hayy Moore
Published and Unpublished
(many to appear in The Ecstatic Exchange Series)

Dawn Visions (published by City Lights, 1964)
Burnt Heart/Ode to the War Dead (published by City Lights, 1972)
This Body of Black Light Gone Through the Diamond (printed by Fred Stone, Cambridge, Mass, 1965)
On The Streets at Night Alone (1965?)
All Hail the Surgical Lamp (1967)
States of Amazement (1970)

Abdallah Jones and the Disappearing-Dust Caper (published by The Ecstatic Exchange/Crescent Series, 2006)
'Ala ud-Deen and the Magic Lamp
The Chronicles of Akhira (1981) (published by Zilzal Press with Typoglyphs by Karl Kempton, 1986)
Mouloud (1984) (A Zilzal Press chapbook, 1995)
Man is the Crown of Creation (1984)
The Look of the Lion (The Parabolas of Sight) (1984)
The Desert is the Only Way Out (completed 4/21/84) (Zilzal Press chapbook, 1985)
Atomic Dance (1984) (am here books, 1988)
Outlandish Tales (1984)
Awake as Never Before (12/26/84) (Zilzal Press chapbook, 1993)
Glorious Intervals (1/1/85) (Zilzal Press chapbook, ?)
Long Days on Earth/Book I (1/28 – 8/30/85)
Long Days on Earth/Book II (Hayy Ibn Yaqzan)
Long Days on Earth/Book III (1/22/86)
Long Days on Earth/Book IV (1986)
The Ramadan Sonnets (Long Days on Earth/Book V) (5/9 – 6/11/86) Published by Jusoor/City Lights Books, 1996) (Republished as Ramadan Sonnets by The Ecstatic Exchange, 2005)
Long Days on Earth/Book VI (6-8/30/86)
Holograms (9/4/86 – 3/26/87)
History of the World (The Epic of Man's Survival) (4/7 – 6/18/87)
Exploratory Odes (6/25 – 10/18/87)
The Man at the End of the World (11/11 – 12/10/87)

The Perfect Orchestra (3/30 – 7/25/88)
Fed from Underground Springs (7/30 – 11/23/88)
Ideas of the Heart (11/27/88 – 5/5/89)
New Poems (scattered poems, out of series, from 3/24 – 8/9/89)
Facing Mecca (5/16 – 11/11/89)
A Maddening Disregard for the Passage of Time (11/17/89 – 5/20/90)
The Heart Falls in Love with Visions of Perfection (6/15/90 – 6/2/91)
Like When You Wave at a Train and the Train Hoots Back at You (Farid's Book) (6/11 – 7/26/91) (Published by The Ecstatic Exchange, 2008)
Orpheus Meets Morpheus (8/1/91– 3/14/92)
The Puzzle (3/21/92 – 8/17/93)
The Greater Vehicle (10/17/93 – 4/30/94)
A Hundred Little 3-D Pictures (5/14/94 – 9/11/95)
The Angel Broadcast (9/29 – 12/17/95)
Mecca/Medina Time-Warp (12/19/95 – 1/6/96) (Published as a Zilzal Press chapbook, 1996)
Miracle Songs for the Millennium (1/20 – 10/16/96)
The Blind Beekeeper (11/15/96 – 5/30/97) (Published 2002 by Jusoor/Syracuse University Press)
Chants for the Beauty Feast (6/3 – 10/28/97)
You Open a Door and it's a Starry Night (10/29/97 – 5/23/98) (Published by The Ecstatic Exchange, 2009)
Salt Prayers (5/29 – 10/24/98) (Published by The Ecstatic Exchange, 2005)
Some (10/25/98 – 4/25/99)
Flight to Egypt (5/1 – 5/16/99)
I Imagine a Lion (5/21 – 11/15/99) (Published by The Ecstatic Exchange, 2006)
Millennial Prognostications (11/25/99 – 2/2/2000) (Published by The Ecstatic Exchange, 2009)
The Book of Infinite Beauty (2/4 – 10/8/2000)
Blood Songs (10/9/2000 – 4/3/2001)
The Music Space (4/10 – 9/16/2001) (Published by The Ecstatic Exchange, 2007)
Where Death Goes (9/20/2001 – 5/1/2002)
The Flame of Transformation Turns to Light (99 Ghazals Written in English) (5/14 – 8/21/2002) (Published by The Ecstatic Exchange, 2007)

Through Rose-Colored Glasses (7/22/2002 – 1/15/2003) (Published by The Ecstatic Exchange, 2007)
Psalms for the Broken-Hearted (1/22 – 5/25/2003) (Published by The Ecstatic Exchange, 2006)
Hoopoe's Argument (5/27 – 9/18/03)
Love is a Letter Burning in a High Wind (9/21 – 11/6/2003) (Published by The Ecstatic Exchange, 2006)
Laughing Buddha/Weeping Sufi (11/7/2003 – 1/10/2004) (Published by The Ecstatic Exchange, 2005)
Mars and Beyond (1/20 – 3/29/2004) (Published by The Ecstatic Exchange, 2005)
Underwater Galaxies (4/5 – 7/21/2004) (Published by The Ecstatic Exchange, 2007)
Cooked Oranges (7/23/2004 – 1/24/2005 (Published by The Ecstatic Exchange, 2007)
Holiday from the Perfect Crime (1/25 – 6/11/2005)
Stories Too Fiery to Sing Too Watery to Whisper (6/13 – 10/24/2005)
Coattails of the Saint (10/26/2005 – 5/10/2006) (Published by The Ecstatic Exchange, 2006)
In the Realm of Neither (5/14/2006 – 11/12/06) (Published by The Ecstatic Exchange, 2008)
Invention of the Wheel (11/13/06 – 6/10/07)
The Sound of Geese Over the House (6/15 – 11/4/07)
The Fire Eater's Lunchbreak (11/11/07 – 5/19/2008) (Published by The Ecstatic Exchange, 2008)
Sparks Off the Main Strike (5/24/2008 – 1/10/2009)

www.ingramcontent.com/pod-product-compliance
Lightning Source LLC
Chambersburg PA
CBHW032039150426
43194CB00006B/348